D1395551

PUTTING LIFE TOGETHER AGAIN

Putting
Life
Together
Again

Robert V. Ozment

FLEMING H. REVELL COMPANY
WESTWOOD · NEW JERSEY

To the four people
with whom I shared my childhood,
and whose love will always be
among my treasured possessions—
      Geraldine
      Buford
      Lon
      Floyd

Preface

ONE DAY A woman with whom I had been counseling phoned me. Her voice revealed, in some measure, the agony of her heart. "I just want to thank you," she said, "for all you have done to help me. But I am going to take my life."

I talked to her and prayed with her. I told her that even though she might feel utterly defeated, God had the answer to the problems that plagued her life.

That philosophy is basic in this book. God *does* have the answers to all the problems we face. There are times when we feel that the future holds nothing for us but misery and disappointment; yet I am confident that with God we can face the future and triumph over whatever tomorrow brings.

The contents of this book have grown out of personal experience, sermon preparation, and counseling with a host of people who have failed to find in life the glow that keeps us steady and gives fresh meaning to our existence. I have walked through some deep valleys and dark nights with those who have known defeat, sorrow, despair, and disappointment as they searched for new hope, renewed strength, and a light of faith. In unnumbered hundreds of lives we have found the hope and strength and faith that brought new life to those who were ready to give up. In some cases where we failed to find the spiritual fortitude lonely souls so desperately needed, the fault was our own, not God's. Sometimes we so completely surround ourselves with selfishness and gloom that we fail to see the warm lights of the Father's house.

The dedication page of the little book *Triumph Over Tragedy*, written by Iona Henry and Frank S. Mead, expresses a part of the theology that is the basis for this book. It reads: "To Dad Henry, who came to meet me in the valley with God's lantern in his hand." None of us can avoid the dark valleys, but in every one of them we can see the path by the light of God's lantern. This light pierces every disappointment, penetrates every cloud of despair, and shines through all our gloom. No matter how lonely the road, we never walk alone. The word of the Lord brought courage to Joshua: "Be strong and of a good courage; be not afraid, neither be thou dismayed: for the Lord thy God is with thee whithersoever thou goest" (JOSHUA 1:9).

To believe that God is unable to help us over the rough places in life is to deny His sovereignty. To give up without first trying to find in God the solutions to our problems reflects lack of faith. The gospel as recorded in the New Testament reveals the faith and courage we must possess if we are to be victorious over the frets and cares of life. Truly, this is a message of hope. It tells us that we can overcome the world and that our sins can be forgiven. It proclaims God's marvelous grace and His everlasting mercy. If we walk with God, we can be triumphant.

It is my hope that those who read this little volume will find in its pages a flickering light of hope for every dark night, a faith that dispels darkness, and God—for to know Him, to believe in Him, and to pray for His will is to live fully.

Contents

1

When Fear

Invades Your Life

TODAY THERE IS probably more written about the subject of "fear" than about any other theme. In spite of this, our mental hospitals have long waiting lists of persons who need immediate attention and professional help. I sometimes feel that we have taken a rather flippant and unwise approach in dealing with fear.

In the first place, we have not always clearly defined the different types of fear. We have failed, for example, to distinguish the vast difference between foolish fears and intelligent concerns. In the second place, most of us have been guilty of painting a picture of fear which represents it as man's greatest enemy. I think an objective analysis of our fears would reveal that this is only partially true; however, it would also present evidence of the value of fear.

Finally, we have written and talked about "Dismiss Your Fears," "How to Conquer Fear," "Steps Out of Fear," "Getting Rid of Fear"—all aimed at promoting the elimination of fear from the human mind. I do not discredit this altogether, no doubt a lot of good can be accomplished from this approach. At the same time we must recognize that this is not the answer to many of our fears. Indeed, it could prove to be a very dangerous method. I have a feeling that we ought to be telling people that some fears can be wise and valuable traveling companions. On the other hand, needless fear can ruin a stalwart soul.

In our weaker moments we may long for a life of ease and comfort; yet when a man straightens his shoulders and stands to his full height, he wants to be challenged. Lack of challenge has been the weight that has kept many a person walking the low roads in education, health, and business, as well as in the matter of morality.

Our approach should include another philosophy: "You Can Take It," "Stand Like a Man," "Learn to Live With Your Fears," "Use Your Fears." Is this not the approach Jesus used? He never promised a life of ease. He talked about suffering, struggle, opposition, and the brutal way men would treat Him. The price of being a disciple was emphasized: a follower had to desert self and have the courage to pick up a cross.

Ever since the beginning of civilization, men have lived under the constant threat of various fears: some are afraid of the past, others are afraid of the future; some are afraid to stand still, others are afraid to march forward.

There was a time when men were afraid because they lacked knowledge. They were afraid of the sea and stars because they were woefully lacking in information about them. Today the situation has often reversed itself. For example, we are filled with fear of atomic bombs because we know something of the threat they hold for civilization. We are afraid of any nuclear weapons because we understand the extent of their horrible destructive power.

Over a generation ago a British publisher asked several laymen to write some sermons to be published under the title, *If I Could Preach Only Once.* Among those invited to write was the late Gilbert Chesterton, an English journalist and author. "If I had only one sermon to preach," wrote Chesterton, "it would be a sermon against fear." The world needs to hear a sermon against the trivial fears that keep us tense and nervous. I believe Jesus would approve of this sort of message.

We all know what it means to be afraid; it is about as common as life itself. Fear is contagious, too. I remember when I was a lad and we lived in a little house in the midst of towering pines. Late one evening heavy dark clouds covered the sky; a strong wind began to blow and the tall pines swayed under the strain. I could see a bit of concern on my mother's face and I remember my dad looking out the front door and saying, "It looks like it might be a bad storm. Those pines are likely to snap under the pressure of such a strong wind." I did not become afraid until my father told my brothers and me to get under the bed. When we asked why he wanted us to do that, he explained that it would be the safest place for us in case one of the big pines crashed into our house. I was not afraid of the storm until I discovered that my dad was afraid for our safety.

There are some things we should know about fear. First, most of our fears are learned. Many psychologists tell us that a child comes into the world with only two inborn fears: he is afraid of falling, and he is afraid of loud sounds. Yet someone figured out a list of several hundred different fears that are common to adult men—we do not inherit them; they are learned from others and through our personal experience.

One lesson modern man must learn—if he is to fulfill his purpose to any degree of effectiveness—is that there is a difference between foolish fears and fears which denote wisdom. For example, it is totally irrational to be afraid of a harmless little snake; but it would be the height of stupidity to cuddle a rattlesnake.

It is estimated by some that about ninety percent of our fears never come to pass. This means that most of our fears have no real basis in reality. If we had the ability to distinguish between those that have a real basis and those that do not, we could save our nervous systems a lot of strain and be able to handle more effectively the ten percent of our fears that need our attention.

Another thing we should keep in mind is the fact that we cannot escape fear. I have known a lot of stalwart men during my life, including some who were decorated for bravery. Yet, all of these men were quick to admit that they had crossed the chasm of fear many times. Fear is a universal language that is understood in the jungle of uncivilized men as well as in the cultured and refined community of a university.

Finally, we ought to remember that fear can be mastered. You do not have to live as a defeated victim of fear. God will not permit His children to live in a room under the power of forces that will ultimately destroy all that is good and worthwhile in their personalities. He will provide them with the power to overcome such enemies.

The fact that some of our fears have no real basis is illustrated very clearly in the life of a man I know. He was very much afraid that he had cancer, and once the idea got hold of his mind, his body was racked with pain. He told me one day that he knew he was dying of cancer. He became a chronic patient, and went to several noted physicians who told him they could find nothing physically wrong. As soon as the man was convinced of the fact that he did not have cancer, his pain went away. Nevertheless, my friend spent several months being afraid of the unreal.

Our little son Randall has a book with a story about a small kitten who was afraid of almost everything. Life was miserable for her: she would not play in the barnyard near the horse because she was afraid the horse would step on her; she refused to go into the barn and get her saucer of milk because she was afraid of the bull's horns; she was afraid to go near a little mouse because she thought it might wrap its long tail around her. The author writes, "She was even afraid of her own shadow—just think of that!" Now, some people become as panic-stricken as that kitten, afraid of the silliest things.

John Dollard tells us that fear has many different names and faces: "It may be called anxiety, apprehension, or restlessness. Sometimes it is a shuddering reality in the face of real danger. At times it appears as boredom. Again it is shown by silence, and yet again by a sudden dampening of the spirit. Turning away often reveals fear. Resentment may disguise it; subservience may conceal it."

Mastering fear is like keeping your garden free from weeds: it is a full-time job. Unless you weed your garden, the weeds will choke out the flowers; unless you keep your mind free from foolish fears, they will rob you of everything worthwhile. You must go into the mind each day and uproot some of your fears, or they will take over.

Fear has two sides. One is a negative side that causes distress and harmful effects to the personality. We must find some effective way to deal with this side of fear. Then there is a positive side, the side which keeps us physically and spiritually alert, and prevents us from placing our lives in undue danger and our souls in jeopardy. It calls out the best that is within us.

Let's look at the negative side of fear, the fear that can weaken the strong and destroy the beautiful. Negative fear can do five things to us:

1. It places a question mark in the mind, a form of doubt. This kind of fear emphasizes the possibility that we may fail. This should not alarm us; we ought to remember that whenever we begin any task we must face the possibility of failure and defeat as well as success.

Fear is the shortest road I know to utter frustration and confusion. One way to make failure inevitable is to magnify the thought that you will probably fail; convince yourself that you cannot complete a task, and you will surely fail.

2. Negative fear destroys our effectiveness. Recently I interviewed some applicants for a position and I was amazed to discover what fear can do to a person. For example, one lady was obviously frightened, so I began the interview by asking her some simple questions, thinking that she might regain her poise and confidence. The longer she stayed, the more nervous and tense she became. She had come to the interview with a very high recommendation, yet she became the victim of merciless fear. She turned red, then white, and became so upset that she failed to answer my questions clearly and correctly.

I know an intelligent man who went to take a written examination for a new position. Fear first put a seed of negative thinking in his mind and finally it destroyed his effectiveness. He failed to pass the examination, yet he knew all the answers. He took the same test again a few weeks later and passed it with a very high score. The first time, fear mastered him; the second time, he mastered his fear.

3. Negative fear robs us of our self-confidence. There is a delightful story in the Old Testament which illustrates the truth of this statement. Elijah had been successful in dealing with the prophets of Baal, but when he heard the threats of Jezebel, the pagan wife of King Ahab, he lost his courage and faith and

became afraid. Elijah ran away, and self-pity became a great force in his life.

4. Negative fear distorts truth. When truth becomes blurred we lose our perspective of things in both the physical and spiritual realms. Fear of the dark causes common objects to take on grotesque shapes and become monsters. Fear of disapproval causes one to feel he is being criticized every time he sees a group of his friends talking.

When we lived in Havana, Cuba, some burglars came for a brief visit one night. My wife and I were sleeping in an upstairs bedroom when we were awakened by two men trying to open the back door. I opened an upstairs window directly over their heads and was about to aim a couple of coconuts down upon them when they left in a hurry. For several nights after that experience, every time I heard the rustle of the palms in the gentle breeze it sounded like someone trying to force his way in through the back door.

5. Once fear has planted a question mark in the mind, destroyed our effectiveness, robbed us of our confidence, or distorted truth, it naturally follows that we become its slave, and therefore it is the master of our lives. I am convinced that a lot of people talk themselves into failure and nervous disorders when they might have talked themselves into success and health.

One of my good friends works as a supervisor with a company that manufactures household cleaning equipment. This company has had an amazing record of success in sales and one day I asked my friend how he accounted for it. He told me several reasons but among them he said, "We go out every day believing that people need our products, and we have confidence in ourselves." Then he told me about one salesman who was so self-confident that he sold a number of hair brushes to bald-headed men!

When fear masters our lives it directs our future; that is to say, it determines our activities. At this level, life is no longer a challenge, but an endurance test. It means the end of progress and the beginning of decay.

One day Jesus told a parable about a man who was taking a vacation, or perhaps going on a business trip. At any rate, the man called his employees together and told them he was leaving them in charge of the work. He gave each man a number of things to do, dividing the chores according to each man's ability to do them.

After many weeks the employer returned and each workman gave an account of his efforts. The first two men came to the owner with pride and told of their success; they were filled with enthusiasm and confidence. But the man who had received only a small share of the responsibility had failed—miserably. From the very beginning he tried to make excuses; he was unwilling to admit that his failure was his own fault. It is easy to place the blame for our failures on someone else, and this man began, "I knew thee that thou art an hard man, reaping where thou hast not sown, and gathering where thou hast not strawed" (MATTHEW 25:24). It was not long, however, until the real reason for his failure was evident: "I was afraid," he admitted. Fear had mastered his life and paralyzed his efforts. It happens today to many people. We let fear grow in our lives until it becomes an unmanageable monster.

I know a man who is very successful in his work and holds a responsible position. One day he told me that he had always had a secret desire to become a physician. I knew that he had had both the ability and the opportunity to attend medical school. "Why," I asked, "didn't you go to medical school?" "I was afraid to try," was his reply. "I was afraid I would fail." He had let his fears master his life and shatter a great ambition.

There is another side of fear that we ought to analyze: the positive side. This kind of fear is one of our best friends, and can do several important things for us if we employ it:

1. Positive fear is a guardian angel over our physical existence. This is why we are wise to teach our children to fear some things. A little child would not know enough to be afraid of a red-hot stove, so we take every precaution to teach him the danger of heat and fire. Small children are not usually afraid of water; therefore it is our responsibility to warn them of the hazards.

Animals are supplied with a generous supply of fear which helps keep them alive. Suppose all the rabbits in this country decided to have a convention, the purpose of which was to talk about their problems with the hunter and the hound. Let us suppose that the featured speaker was Mr. Cotton Tail, Ph. D. in psychology—his subject: "Fear Is Useless." Imagine the speaker saying, "You rabbits don't need to be afraid of a shotgun and a hound! This reveals your immaturity. You rabbits must be brave. Courage must be your motto. Stand up and fight the hound and defy the shotgun!" That wouldn't even make good rabbit sense. It may be all right to talk like that at a convention, but the philosophy wouldn't work out in a field when an honest-to-goodness rabbit faced the shotgun and the hound. God provided the rabbit with a powerful stimulant that enables him to run for his life at the first scent of impending danger. Because of fear, he manages to stay alive.

In the sense that fear protects us, we must admit that it is our friend. Therefore we do not wish to banish all fear—that would mean utter chaos for the human family.

2. Positive fear serves as a guard to moral decency. A story that came out of World War II illustrates what I mean. It seems that a group of soldiers who had been fighting for several months were brought back for a few days of rest and relaxation near one of the large European cities. On the first night away from the front lines some of the boys decided to "live it up." They discussed their plans for the night while they were dressing to go out. One of the young soldiers made no attempt to dress, and it was obvious that he was not going out. When asked by some of his buddies why he wasn't going with them, he remarked, "I have asked a girl back home to marry me. She promised she would, as soon as I return from this awful war. I promised her that I would keep myself clean and make every effort to be worthy of her love." At that moment the other men thought about their loved ones across the seas; some thought of mothers, others of sisters, still others thought of wives and sweethearts. Then they decided to go to a good restaurant and see a movie. The fear of betraying a promise to stay morally clean deterred what might have been a tragic night for the souls of those young soldiers.

I would be the first to admit that fear is not the best motive for maintaining standards that are morally acceptable. Yet, in many instances it is the only guard some people will obey. Many people would be guilty of betraying the sacred vows of marriage if they thought they could "get away with it." The fear of losing something more valuable keeps them faithful and curbs the evil appetite of the flesh.

Sometimes I am in a hurry. I guess if I were to be absolutely honest I should say that I stay in a hurry. I have to hurry in order to accomplish the work I need to do each day. There are times when I am tempted to drive my car excessively fast in order to keep an appointment. I suppose, too, there are days when I would drive at a greater speed than the legal limit, if it were not for fear. I am afraid of at least three things: I might injure some innocent person, I might hurt myself, and finally, I might be caught and fined by law enforcement officers.

Fear is the motivating force which makes me do many things that I do not enjoy doing. For example, I do not like to buy insurance for my automobile; however, I would be afraid to drive without it. Whenever I go fishing or boating in a large body of water I always wear a life jacket. I do not enjoy wearing it; I do so because I am afraid of being drowned in case of an accident.

3. Positive fear helps us develop human personality to its full potential. Some time ago I received a letter from a lady who was disturbed about a phrase she had seen in the Bible. "What," she wrote, "does it mean to 'fear God'?" This certainly cannot mean that we are to be afraid of or to dread God. Once Jesus said to His disciples, "And fear not them which kill the body, but are not able to kill the soul: but rather fear him which is able to destroy both soul and body in hell" (MATTHEW 10:28). Of course, Jesus was talking about God, because God is the only One who has the power to destroy both body and soul.

Moses, in talking to the Hebrews, said, "And now, Israel, what doth the Lord thy God require of thee, but to fear the Lord thy God, to walk in all his ways, and to love him, and to serve the Lord thy God with all thy heart, and with all thy soul, To keep the commandments of the Lord, and his statutes, which I command thee this day for thy good?" (DEUTERONOMY 10:12-13).

The question remains, "How shall we fear God?" To fear God means to stand before God in awe, with a sense of profound reverence. To fear God means to love, respect, and obey His commandments.

The fear of God releases us from the fear of man. I am filled with fear whenever there is a break in my relationship to God as a true son. This kind of fear makes me want to please God and obey His laws; it sends me back to my knees and stirs a desire to repent of my sins. This kind of fear makes us speak up on behalf of righteousness; it makes us afraid to display cowardice in the face of evil.

As Christians, we must let the world know where we stand. Back in my seminary days I heard a story about a blind and almost deaf woman who never missed a Sunday in church. This seemed strange to some, in view of the fact that she could neither see nor hear anything that went on during the service. One day someone asked her, "Why do you come to church?" and she replied, "To show which side I am on." That is reason enough for anyone.

When the Nazi soldiers marched into Norway the Christian churches fought the corrupt and evil philosophy of Hitler. Eivind Berggrav, Bishop of Oslo during the tragic period, was ordered to appear before Quisling, a ruthless man, whose task was to quell all opposition to Nazism. In one of his verbal attacks upon the brave and dedicated bishop, Quisling shouted, "You triple traitor, you deserve having your head chopped off!" The bishop calmly replied, "Well, here I am." As Ernest Tittle said, "Fear of God drove out fear of Quisling. . . . he [Bishop Berggrav] was not afraid to die because he was afraid to betray a sacred trust."

No one would deny that fear is a problem common to all of us. Most people want to know how to use their fears instead of being used by their fears. Jesus knew the fears of a real world: He was rejected, criticized, and crucified; He felt the heavy weight of the cross long before He started up Calvary's hill. In spite of this, Jesus continued to tell people over and over, "Be not afraid," and "Fear not." He did not tell people, "There is no real cause for fear." Jesus did not attempt to hide the hard facts of life. The disciples were warned from the beginning that they would probably be hated, persecuted, and even killed for their faith. But in the midst of it all, Jesus encouraged them by saying, "Be not afraid."

We have not been able to abandon all our fears. I dare say we shall never outgrow them. Let us suppose that courage, love, patience, knowledge, and fear were to get together for a banquet. Fear sits at the head of the table, and the guests begin to discuss the importance of each guest to the human family. Courage says, "If man had to do without one of us, which would be missed the least?" And it is decided that each should make a short speech to justify his existence. Courage is first: "The world could never get along without me. Society must have someone who has the courage to speak for truth. Righteousness could never survive without me." Love speaks next: "Unless there is love, life loses its meaning and purpose. I am the crowning virtue of life. I make life worth the struggle. I determine the destiny of men." Then Patience speaks, "Without me the people of the world would live in utter chaos. I am the key to success. Men do not succeed overnight; when they fail, I send them back to their tasks." Knowledge is next: "I am the channel through which man learns about himself, his world, others, and God. I am the key to light, truth, and worthwhile living." What will Fear say? How can Fear ever justify its presence? "Most people," Fear begins, "have misunderstood me. They have looked upon me as an enemy, but really I am a friend. I am God's gift to man. I stand guard over man's spirit and his soul. I help guide him to the abundant life." All the others join in a mighty chorus and shout, "Fear is our friend! Fear is our friend!"

J. Wallace Hamilton said, "We are motivated by fear every day of our lives, and moved by fear, we do many good and constructive things. That is exactly what fear is for: it is the friend of order, the buttress of morality, the ally of the kingdom of God." The writer of Proverbs said, "The fear of the Lord is a fountain of life . . ." (14:27).

What can we do about our fears? First, we can analyze them and see what it is that makes us afraid. I believe we will discover that most of our fears have no real basis. It was Jesus who said, "And ye shall know the truth, and the truth shall make you free" (JOHN 8:32). The truth about many of our fears will set us free.

Unfounded fear came to the disciples. Once they were in the midst of the sea and Jesus had remained ashore to pray. The wind was contrary and the disciples were busily engaged in rowing the boat. Then Jesus approached and the disciples looked up and saw Him. They were filled with fear. They thought their eyes were playing tricks on them. They decided it was a spirit and cried out. Jesus immediately assured them that there was no need to be afraid: "Be of good cheer: it is I; be not afraid" (MARK 6:50). When Jesus entered the little boat the disciples were amazed. I can imagine the shame on their faces. Peter must have said, "How silly it was for us to be afraid! We should have guessed that it was You, Lord."

Several weeks ago I was walking from an airlines terminal to board a plane. It was a long walk and a stewardess who was to work on the flight was walking beside me. She remarked, "I am so afraid, I don't know what to do."

"Why are you afraid?" I asked.

"This is my first flight," she answered. I tried to assure her that her fear was unfounded. She had been trained for her job and the plane had been checked out. At the end of the flight she said, "You were right. There was no need to be afraid."

Some months ago a young man came to see me. He had finished college and had taken several months of special training for a certain position. "I am nervous," he said; "in fact, I am afraid I will fail in this new job."

I asked, "What makes you feel afraid?"

"I don't know," he answered.

"Well, let's look at the picture," I suggested. "You have everything in your favor. You have finished college and have had some special training for this work. The people for whom you are going to work will be glad to see you, and you will be doing them a service. They believe that you can do the work. Why be afraid?"

It was wonderful to see the renewed confidence in the young man's face. "Well," he said, "when you look at it that way, I guess it is silly to be afraid." As he went to the door, he said, "If I can just keep those things in mind, I won't be afraid." The first six months on his new job have shown that young man that he had no real reason to be fearful.

After analyzing your fears, pray about them. When Jesus was troubled in the Garden, He prayed. I sometimes pray this little prayer: "God give me the grace to walk unafraid through the shadows of groundless fears, and the wisdom to be afraid of those things which profane virtues, pollute character, and stain the soul." Sincere prayer can turn your fears into stepping-stones.

Jesus lay asleep in a little boat while His disciples tried to keep the boat from being tossed about by mighty waves. The disciples were doing all they could do, but that was not enough. There are times when we feel as they felt—the storm is so big and our boats are so small. No matter what we do, our efforts seem inadequate. The disciples did the only thing they could: they called upon the Master for help. When Jesus saw the waves and sensed the fear in the hearts of the disciples He said, "Peace, be still." At His command the wind ceased to blow and the storm was over. Well, we do not have the power simply to say to our fears, "Peace, be still," and make them disappear, but we can put our trust in God's care. Jesus gave us the secret of how to live above our fears. After the storm abated He looked at His disciples and said, "Why are ye so fearful? how is it that ye have no faith?" (MARK 4:40).

You can live above your fears if you believe in the God Christ revealed unto us. The secret of the victorious life our Lord lived was His complete trust in God. Jesus knew, beyond the possibility of doubt, that God is good and can be trusted.

What is His God like? First, Jesus knew that God is equal to any situation in life; that is, God is greater than our problems and fears. Then, God can be trusted. When we commit ourselves to Him we need not be afraid; He will keep His word. It is the still small voice of God that whispers to us throughout life, "Do not be afraid."

We hear the preacher talk about God on Sunday, but frequently our belief in God is mechanical. We believe in Him as we believe in the sun. We see the sun, and feel its warmth. Scientists have told us that the sun is about ninety-three million miles away from the earth, but that is not much information compared with all there is to know about the solar system. Still, we believe that the sun will rise and set each day.

We accept the fact that God exists because we reason that this marvelous and intelligent universe must have a wise Creator behind it. Surely such order and beauty could not have come out of chaos or nothing. Simply to accept the fact that God exists, however, is not sufficient to enable us to live above our fears. A man must move from an intellectual realm, in which he merely tips his hat to God, into a realm of faith and trust. Here he walks with God. I sometimes wonder if we are using our knowledge to the best advantage when I read what William James had to say about prehistoric man: "Plunged in darkest ignorance, preyed upon by hideous and grotesque superstitions, he nevertheless clung steadfastly to the faith that existence in any form is better than non-existence, and so rescued triumphantly from the jaws of an ever-imminent destruction the torch of life."

I, for one, would rather place my soul in the keeping of one who can neither read nor write, yet who in all of his life reflects a profound faith in the goodness and wisdom of a loving and kind God, than to commit my soul to the influence of some noted scholar whose intellect is internationally acclaimed, yet who cannot make up his mind whether or not he believes in God.

"Faith is required of thee," wrote Thomas á Kempis, "and a sincere life, not loftiness of intellect, nor deepness in the mysteries of God." Fears will surge up within our souls. We cannot keep them from our minds, but through faith we can live above them. We need a faith like the one expressed in a little poem by Ella Wheeler Wilcox:

> With the rising of the sun,
> Think of your life as just begun.
> The past has shrived and buried deep
> All yesterdays; there let them sleep.
>
> Concern yourself with but today,
> Woo it, and teach it to obey
> Your will and wish. Since time began
> Today has been the friend of man;

But in his blindness and his sorrow,
He looks to yesterday and tomorrow.
You, and today! a soul sublime,
And the great pregnant hour of time,
With God himself to bind the twain!
Go forth, I say—attain, attain!
With God himself to bind the twain!

A faith that cannot ride the bitter waves of fear on the sea of life is like a ship that is no longer seaworthy. A shallow faith cannot keep the waves of fear from dashing us to pieces.

Bray Booth, the son of Dr. and Mrs. Edwin P. Booth, was killed in the service of his country during World War II. Bray was a brilliant young man, with a mind intent on serving humanity. He entered Harvard University at the age of seventeen, and was inducted into the army in 1943. He volunteered for paratroop service and about nineteen months later he was killed in action. The War Department at first sent a "missing in action" telegram; there was still hope in the hearts of Dr. and Mrs. Booth, and twice each day the doctor went to the post office, hoping to receive word that Bray was still alive. One day the final telegram came, blotting out all hope and telling the Booths that Bray was dead.

We have seen the victory of the final test of faith in many lives. It was reflected again in the lives of the Booths as they received the crushing news. Dr. Booth wrote, "At first the whole world was shaken beneath my feet. Then slowly a few simplicities came steadily before me. God's existence never wavered in my thought." This kind of faith comes from a life that believes with all its heart, mind, and strength in the goodness of God; this faith makes the weary soul give himself completely to God. When we have faith like this, we can live above the fears that perplex us.

When we look at life through the eyes of Christian faith, all things focus on a God whose voice can be heard during life's blackest day, saying, "Be not afraid, because I am with thee."

2

Getting Light
for the Darkness

NO PERSON IN his right mind would deny that these are critical times in which we live. The progress of mankind is threatened by war. We have pulled up our anchors of unwavering integrity in favor of more profits. Some businessmen are asking, "How can we make money and be true to the best we know?"

A few years ago a very promising man came to see me. He had been born with a natural gift for selling and was making money for himself as well as the company for which he worked; his sales force was bringing in more orders than the plant could produce. One day the sales manager called a meeting and immediately after it the young man turned in his resignation. When I asked, "Why?" he replied, "I just couldn't lie to the customer. I have always been taught that this was wrong. The sales manager told us, 'Promise the customer anything, but bring those orders in.' Peace of mind means more than a paycheck to me." The man who fails to live up to the best he knows will soon forget what "the best" really is.

If you could read my mail, or answer my telephone, or sit in my office for one week you would see some of the problems that grip many people. In a recent newspaper column I wrote about the power of God that is available to the lowest, the least, and the last of God's children. I tried to say as clearly as possible that God's presence is adequate to guide us safely through every dark valley. When man faces the future with God, he can be triumphant. By the time that newspaper reached the newsstand a man called me and said, "I have just finished reading your column and I want to ask one question: What can a man do when the whole world seems to be against him and there is no future?" I replied, "Do exactly what Jesus did when He faced Calvary: pray that God's will might be done. Follow the example of the Master as He hung on the cross: He prayed, 'Father, into thy hands I commend my spirit.'" When a person surrenders his will and commits his life to God, he is assured of victory. The ugly crucifixion looked like the end for our Lord, and the disciples thought it spelled utter defeat; but God changed it into victory.

A father who lost his family in a tragic accident prayed, "O God, this valley is deep and dark and I prefer death more than life; but if You've got something else for me to do, give me the strength to take another step and I will take it in faith." This man could find no reason to live. All that he loved was in the past. As I talked with him some years later he confided, "The ache is still in my heart, but God in His infinite wisdom and tender love has brought me safely through." That is always the story if we fully trust Him. To use the words of the Psalmist: "God is our refuge and strength, a very present help in trouble" (46:1).

I have come to believe that hope and purpose are found not in the absence of trouble and sorrow, but in the presence of God. Some folks never sense the presence of God until they come to a place in the path of life where human strength is not enough. Then, one of two things happens: either they are defeated, or they move on in the strength of God. If we move on in God's strength we can proclaim with Robert Louis Stevenson, "There stood at the wheel that unknown steersman whom we call God."

One of my favorite stories in the New Testament is recorded in the Gospels. It describes a multitude of people who had assembled to catch a glimpse of the Master. Jesus looked beyond their garments and searched their hearts. Can you imagine the hurts, sorrows, and disappointments that are buried in the hearts of a crowd of people gathered for any occasion? As an example, let us consider those who read these lines. Some of you have experienced a recent disappointment; your plans have not worked out as you hoped they would. Others are searching for the key to happiness. Some may feel forsaken and alone. Still others, having loved ones who are ill, are anxious about them. Some of you are worried about your children. Some are afraid of the demands of tomorrow. There are those who are struggling under the load of guilt; perhaps you have failed to live up to the best you know and you need forgiveness. Some are lonely; some have financial problems; some are anxious about their health.

When I go to a football game I see a big crowd of people. Often I stop and look at some of them and wonder about the secret hurts they know and the spiritual needs of their lives. Many times I pray for someone who is sitting near me. I ask God to grant unto him the strength he needs to face the battles of life with confidence.

When Jesus saw the crowd He began to search the hearts of individual people and He saw fear and frustration. He immediately knew the needs of those who lingered in that crowd. The Bible tells us that Jesus ". . . was moved with compassion toward them, because they were as sheep not having a shepherd . . ." (MARK 6:43).

It is amazing to discover that Jesus looks into our hearts, and He knows our needs. Not only does He know our needs, but He can supply them. Do you need more strength? Then go to Christ and He will give it to you. Do you need more grace to live the Christian life? Then go to Christ and you can get it. Do you need more understanding, more patience, in your relationships with others? Go to Christ and He will grant them. Do you need more courage and spiritual fortitude to face tomorrow? Go to Christ and they can be yours. No matter what your needs are, they can be met and satisfied in Jesus Christ.

Not only did Jesus have compassion on the crowd, but ". . . he began to teach them many things" (MARK 6:34). I wish the writers of the Gospels had recorded the message Jesus delivered on that occasion. I count it a tremendous loss not to know what our Lord said to those frustrated people.

Of course, it is sheer speculation on my part, but knowing the life of Jesus as we do from the New Testament I have an idea He must have said something like this: "Don't be afraid of life. Put your faith in God and He will sustain you. Bring your sins to Him and He will forgive. Your noble hopes can be achieved, your worthy dreams will someday be fulfilled, and your holy aspirations will be realized if you commit your life to God and trust Him completely. Remember, with God all things are possible."

Jesus is concerned with all our needs. He wants us to be whole in mind and body as well as in spirit. After Jesus had taught the multitude, and when the shadows of the late afternoon were in evidence, the disciples suggested that the crowd be sent home where they could find food. Jesus wanted to minister to their physical needs as well as the needs of their souls; therefore He looked at His disciples and said. "Give them something to eat." The disciples replied, "There isn't that much food available. To feed this multitude would require at least two hundred pennyworth of bread." Jesus asked, "How many loaves do you have?" The disciples found five loaves and two fishes. Jesus then fed the people, and the disciples gathered twelve full baskets over and above that which had been eaten.

It is amazing how difficult and impossible life appears at times. Then, when we seek the help of the Master, everything changes. The disciples looked at the multitude, and the five loaves and two small fishes seemed so meager, so inadequate. Our Lord changed all that, and made the impossible seem easy.

Jesus said, on another occasion, ". . . for with God all things are possible" (MARK 10:27). Don't ever say, "God has given me an impossible task to perform." God never makes an impossible demand of us. You and I are assured of the strength to be victorious in any task God has given us to do. If your burdens appear more than you can bear, take hope and claim the promise of God, that with Him "all things are possible."

Jesus suggested that the disciples take the boat and cross the sea to Bethsaida while He sent the people away. Then He went aside to be alone with His Father in prayer. Perhaps Jesus felt the need of divine direction. Perhaps He wanted to be sure that

His life was in perfect harmony with God's will. Our Lord was keenly aware of His need for constant divine fellowship. Even after the miracle of feeding five thousand people with five loaves and two fishes, Jesus had an inner compulsion to commune with God.

This brings into sharp focus our need for divine fellowship and guidance. Unlike the Master, many of us forget God when we are triumphant. As long as things are going our way we seldom feel an inner desire to go aside and pray. Genuine prayer is not an emergency kit which we use in times of dire stress; it is an attitude of the soul that develops when we walk daily with God.

As the shadows lengthened and the disciples pushed their little boat away from the shore, the sea was calm and things were normal. Then, without warning, the winds arose and the little boat was tossed about. The men were rowing with all their might but even their best did not seem adequate. Life is like that: one day the sun is shining and our hearts are gay, and suddenly the storm comes and our best just isn't enough. When the disciples were at the point of their greatest despair Jesus came walking on the sea and they were filled with fear. Jesus spoke, as He always does, and reassured them.

Matthew tells us that Peter said, "Lord, if it be thou, bid me come unto thee on the water" (14:28). Jesus invited Peter to come to Him, and Peter "walked on the water." This is evidence of what God can do in the life of a person who will trust Him completely. Peter could not walk on the water by his own power, but for a moment God gave Peter divine power through his perfect faith to do that which he could never have accomplished alone.

In this incident we see an important part of God's divine character. When we trust in God He gives us all the strength necessary to become the person He wants us to be. I am not saying that you can perform miracles or walk on the water— and I do not believe that this is essential in reaching the destiny for which God created you. I am saying that no matter what your circumstances in life, if you are sensitive to God He will bring you through the storms to the safety of the divine harbor where the lights of the Father's house burn brightly.

Often we feel compelled to pray, "Lord, take the storms of life away. Cause them to cease; provide a detour around this trouble." We know that God does not always answer our prayers by removing the trouble or causing the storms of circumstance to cease; there are times when the Master stills the storm that is raging within by causing the winds of worry and anxiety to cease. When we open the doors of our hearts and invite Him in, His presence gives us hope, assurance, a sustaining faith, and an enduring fortitude that enables us to hear the Master saying, "My grace is sufficient for thee . . ." (II CORINTHIANS 12:9). You see, there isn't any storm that can descend upon us which cannot be endured when we know that God is near.

I received a telephone call from a wonderful lady who is facing the sunset of life. She told me about her family and how fine her children were. "I know my time on earth is short," she said, "but this does not make me afraid. I have walked with God and He has helped me through many troubles and sorrows. Death does not frighten me. I believe God is good and I know He loves me, and those two beliefs keep me from being afraid." Before she finished she made one request: "Just pray that my faith will be strong and that I will be loyal to God until the end of my earthly journey." I have prayed that prayer, and I believe she will be loyal. She will be loyal—not necessarily because of my prayer, but because of her faith.

Jesus was constantly reminding people to take heart. On several occasions He said, "Be not afraid." Jesus had courage and knew how to face life unafraid, but He also had the ability to impart this courage and confidence to others. In the presence of Jesus people discovered a marvelous peace that kept them from being afraid. Little wonder the sick and troubled thronged Him wherever He went. They wanted the same peace and serenity that He possessed.

Jesus never said, "There isn't anything to be afraid of in life. Keep your chin up and everything will be easy for you. Nothing is going to hurt you." Actually, He said the reverse. Quite clearly He told His followers that they would get into trouble because of Him. The Christians of the first century found it a challenge to follow Jesus. They were cruelly persecuted, and it took Christian fortitude and courage based on faith to stand up and wave the flag of the Christian church. It still does. We would certainly agree that it is not always easy to live the Christian life in this twentieth century. Jesus talked about a cross. ". . . take up the cross, and follow me," He said to one who had asked, ". . . what shall I do that I may inherit eternal life?" (MARK 10:17). Jesus did not try to deceive those who followed Him. He reminded the disciples, "In the world ye shall have tribulation . . ." (JOHN 16:33). Jesus did not say, "In the world you *may* have tribulation"; He said, ". . . ye shall have tribulation. . . ." It would be difficult to misunderstand His words.

Jesus did not leave us hopelessly stranded amidst the tribulations of life. He said, ". . . but be of good cheer; I have overcome the world" (JOHN 16:33). Right in the face of the hard facts of life Jesus urged us to hang on to faith and discard our fears. The disciples were bucking heavy seas and fighting high waves when Jesus said to them, "Why are ye fearful, O ye of little faith?" (MATTHEW 8:26). When Jesus was on His way to heal the sick daughter of Jairus, someone came and said to Jairus, "Thy daughter is dead: why troublest thou the Master any further?" (MARK 5:35). It was then Jesus turned to Jairus and said, "Be not afraid, only believe" (MARK 5:36). Jairus might have responded by saying, "Jesus, didn't You hear the news? My little girl is dead. The one who means so much to me is gone, and You tell me, 'Be not afraid, only believe.'"

The disciples might have answered, "What are You saying? Don't You see these high waves? We are about to lose our lives, and You tell us not to be afraid!" Jesus was saying, in both instances, "As long as you walk with Me, you need not be afraid, because I will sustain you."

Bishop Arthur J. Moore, in *Fight On! Fear Not!*, reminds us that "Christ does not take us out of the battle; He does something better. He gives us trust and triumph in the battle and promises that at the end of the struggle a friendly hand will guide us into the presence of One whose, 'Well done, thou good and faithful servant,' will glorify the battle scars."

I must confess that I become discouraged at times. I am impatient when humanity moves so slowly up the moral ladder. Our scientific progress staggers the imagination, while our spiritual achievement is almost embarrassing. It is almost commonplace to orbit the earth and yet we have failed to learn how to apply the golden rule to business; nor have we learned to understand our neighbors, much less love them. I see much that is dark and evil in our world, but when I stand at the foot of the cross and catch a glimpse of the extent to which God was willing to go to save us, and when I remember the glorious truth of Easter, I go back to my workbench with renewed hope and unwavering assurance that righteousness will one day triumph.

Jesus looked into the face of a world where justice was trampled and goodness was bruised. He saw a lot of things wrong with our world, and He knew that changes were necessary. In spite of all that was wrong with the world into which Jesus came, He was hopeful.

1. Jesus wants us to face life courageously. After the resurrection, when He commissioned His disciples to carry on the work, He was aware that they might be fearful and He assured them of His presence. He was saying to them, "Don't be afraid of life. You are not alone in this venture." Jesus said, ". . . lo, I am with you alway . . ." (MATTHEW 28:20). God's work is not easily accomplished in our world, but with His help we can do all that He expects of us.

Life can be faced successfully. You and I can be victorious, no matter what the circumstances of life. We will not be afraid when we learn to trust God as fully as the old man who prayed, "O Lord, I believe in You, and I know that nothing will come up this day but what You and I can handle it together." Don't be afraid of life; the power of God is available to you.

2. The Lord wants us to see our filthy sins, but He never wants us to conclude that our situation is hopeless. Calvary is powerful enough to cover all our sins.

Some few months ago a lady called and wanted to see me. I gave her an appointment and she came to my office and related a shameful past. Her sins were filthy and her soul was stained. "I am ashamed of myself," she said. "I just can't stand living with myself." Tears filled her eyes and rolled down her cheeks. "Will God forgive me?" she asked. I assured her that God's love was unfathomable and His forgiveness inexhaustible.

I read several passages from the New Testament. Then I

turned to the eighth chapter of John and read her the story of the gentleness of the Master in dealing with one who had been accused of adultery. Jesus saw in that woman's heart not only an ugly deed but a burning desire to be forgiven. He did not embarrass her by asking her to tell Him about the deed. He simply said, "Neither do I condemn thee: go, and sin no more" (JOHN 8:11). Then I turned to the twenty-third chapter of Luke and read the story of the thief dying on the cross. The thief said to Jesus, "Lord remember me when thou comest into thy kingdom. And Jesus said unto him, Verily I say unto thee, To day shalt thou be with me in paradise" (LUKE 23:42-43). Earlier Jesus had said, "I came not to call the righteous, but sinners to repentance" (LUKE 5:32). No life is beyond the power of God to redeem.

3. Jesus did not want us to be afraid of death. I have walked to the side of an open grave many times and read these words of our Lord: "Let not your heart be troubled: ye believe in God, believe also in me. In my Father's house are many mansions: if it were not so, I would have told you" (JOHN 14:12). His resurrection assures us that life is eternal. I often tell people that death is the only door that leads to the Father's house. No one will ever be able to convince me that a God who created us, sustains us, and loves us enough to send His Son up the terrible slopes of Calvary would give us this great gift of life and then deceive us at the end of our earthly journey. Birth is the gateway from the first stage of life to another stage; and death is the gate that frees us from the limitations of earth and ushers us into the spacious living room of God.

Henry Wadsworth Longfellow wrote:

The grave itself is but a covered bridge
Leading from light to light, through a brief darkness.

The idea expresses immortality, but I beg to disagree with that great poet. I do not believe that there will be even a "brief darkness," for we are never out of sight of God. He is, even in death, close enough to hold us by the hand. The Psalmist reminds us that we can never escape God: "If I take the wings of the morning, and dwell in the uttermost parts of the sea; Even there shall thy hand lead me, and thy right hand shall hold me" (139:9-10).

Walter Savage Landor wrote:

> Death stands above me, whispering low—
> I know not what into my ear;
> Of his strange language, all I know
> Is, there is not a word of fear.

The Master waves the flag and gives us the signal to advance, not only in life but in death as well. He wants us to follow Him, and He said, ". . . because I live, ye shall live also" (John 14:19). He mastered life; He conquered death—and so can we.

Jesus did not have an easy existence, but He had a happy life. He was sensitive to the evil around Him, but He was also aware of the presence of God within Him. The outward forces of life could not defeat Him because He was buttressed from within with spiritual braces. How could Jesus face the hard facts of a sinful world with serenity and assurance? What was His secret?

Jesus faced the raging storms of life with an astounding inner peace because He believed in God. Some folks know about God but do not believe in Him. God seems unreasonable to many human minds. Little wonder we live so much of life in valleys of confusion and frustration. I do not mean that one's belief in God will solve every problem of life; but I do mean that unless one believes in God, life is void of meaning. I hasten to add that when one fully believes in the God revealed to us in Christ, all the problems of life can be either endured or solved. H. G. Wells wrote, "Religion is the first thing and the last thing, and until a man has found God he begins at no beginning; he works to no end."

George MacDonald, a Scottish poet, made this astounding observation to the men of his generation: "You are little children sitting on the curbstone hunting in the gutter for things. Behind you is a King's palace, finer than Buckingham. In it your Father sits. But you won't listen. You won't even turn around to look. You just keep on hunting in the gutter for things, and it doesn't matter whether it's rotten vegetables or pennies or shillings you find there. They can't make you happy without your Father."

Are we not guilty of the same thing? Many of us go on living in the gutter, searching for happiness where it is impossible to find it. The emphasis of MacDonald's words should not be placed on the Father in the palace, but upon the fact that we can join Him there. He wants us to live in the palace of love, forgiveness, understanding, and perfect peace.

What Jesus believed about God was significant. He believed that God was both good and wise, and this belief caused Him to trust God fully. The trouble with some of us is that we find it difficult to believe in a God who is greater than our comprehension. A God we could fully understand would not be big enough to do for us what must be done if we are to fulfill our destiny.

J. W. Hawley read these words of the French scientist: "I have swept the universe with my telescope, and I find no God." Mr. Hawley responded, "Of course that is as unreasonable as for me to say, 'I have taken this violin apart. I have examined each piece with my microscope, and I find no music.'" Need any more be said?

There are moments in our lives when we feel that God is far away. As a minister I have seen people who felt that God had forsaken them. Their troubles seemed more than they could bear. What we believe about God during days of sorrow and frustration will make the difference.

Walter Russell Bowie, in his book *Remembering Christ,* relates the moving story of two soldiers who stood together on a bloody battlefield. One man, gazing into the zone referred to as "No man's land," observed curtly, "Look at that! Where is God now?" The other looked at the wounded and the dead lying all around. Then, in the heat of the battle, he saw the stretcher-bearers going after the wounded. Pointing in that direction, he said, "He is there. There is God." Yes, God is wherever men suffer. He is everywhere there is human need. Do you need Him? If so, call upon Him and He will help you.

3

From Failure

to Victory

NO PERSON ENJOYS being defeated. Basically, we all want the respect of others as well as our self-respect, and a sense of being "somebody" is important to us.

A young man was caught robbing a bank some few months ago, and during the interrogation the police officers asked, "Why did you want to rob the bank?" The young man replied, "I just wanted to be somebody." He went on to explain that he had been out of work for several weeks and didn't have any money. He felt utterly defeated. "I just got to thinking," he said, "if I had some money in my pocket I would feel like somebody." I know a lot of people who will tell you that money is not the answer to man's deep longings. It is not the treasures on earth that make us happy, but the treasures that cannot be assailed by moths, ruined by rust, or stolen by thieves.

Life is a constant struggle. The battles crowd in upon us; there are financial hardships, sickness, sorrow, fears of many types, and moments of defeat. There are times when it is difficult to see any light of hope in the future. Every person comes to the place in life where he feels defeated. I want to suggest three things for us to remember when we face what appear to be unconquerable problems:

1. "What shall we then say to these things?" (ROMANS 8:31). How will we face the perplexing problems of life? What

are we going to do about the things that seem to hold us back and defeat us? Our attitude toward life will defeat us much faster than our burdens. I know some people who have given up in defeat when the common storms of life descended upon them; I know others who have faced what appears to be more than their share of heartaches, yet they have managed to keep a Christian perspective of life.

Paul took the attitude that we are not alone. He said, "For I am persuaded, that neither death, nor life, . . . shall be able to separate us from the love of God . . ." (ROMANS 8:38-39). Those who have their faith firmly anchored in the goodness of God never fail to pass successfully through the dark ways of life into the sunshine of God's measureless love.

I have seen many people triumph over their sorrow because of a Christian attitude. Recently a man sat in my office after learning that his father was dying. We prayed together and I asked God to give the family courage and hope for the hours ahead. Instead of blaming God for his loss, this man said, "We are mighty thankful that God let him stay with us so long. We hate to give him up but we know God has been good to us." He was able to count his blessings, even through tears of sorrow.

Recently I talked to a lovely lady who will be going to visit an open grave before many days. She said, "God knows where I am and I know where He is." I see a beautiful relationship in that statement. She was saying, "I have walked across the years with God and I have tried to be faithful to Him. I am not afraid to pass through the lonely valley of death because I know God holds my hand."

2. Paul said, "If God be for us, who can be against us?" (ROMANS 8:31). He was urging us to look at the problems of life against the backdrop of God's power. We need to take our minds off our problems and think about the power that is available to us. What enemy can prevail over us if we march with God? You may be certain that no situation in life is hopeless, because God's power is greater than all the burdens, heartaches, problems, and sins that man can know.

3. Let us remember the answer Paul received to his prayer asking God to remove his thorn in the flesh: "My grace is sufficient for thee . . ." (II CORINTHIANS 12:9). Little wonder Paul preached the power of God! When Paul said, "I can do all

things through Christ which strengtheneth me" (PHILIPPIANS 4:13), that was not mere philosophical theory or theological conjecture. Those words did not fall like pious platitudes from the lips of one who spent most of his life in an ivory tower. Paul was speaking out as one who had spent most of his life on the battlefield. He knew what it was like to be despised, forsaken, beaten, shipwrecked, cast into prison. He knew the power of Rome and the demands of the Christian life. He had discovered something else: he knew the power of God, and that made the difference.

Let us face life fortified with the knowledge that God never forgets us. The Psalmist wrote, "The Lord is merciful and gracious, slow to anger, and plenteous in mercy" (103:8). He even suggested that God's mercy never ends; it is from everlasting to everlasting upon them that fear Him. When sorrow comes and loneliness lingers, we can be sure that God will not place upon us burdens that cannot be borne or sorrows that cannot be endured. The Psalmist said, "For he knoweth our frame; he remembereth that we are dust" (103:14). God will never ask us to do the impossible.

Those who have walked on the mountain peaks of achievement, enjoying the thrill of success, have also stumbled through the valleys of disappointment and hard work. In a child's reader there is a story of a small lad who shoveled through a large drift of snow. When asked how such a small boy could shovel through such a tremendous drift of snow the lad replied, "By keeping at it, sir." How true! The problems of life are solved by "keeping at them."

Robert Browning wrote, "If I stoop into a dark tremendous sea of cloud—It is but for a time. I press God's lamp—Close to my breast; its splendor soon or late—Will pierce the gloom: I shall emerge one day." It took Edward Gibbon twenty years to write *The Decline and Fall of the Roman Empire.*

While working in his laboratory at two o'clock one morning, Thomas Edison had a smile on his face. An assistant, seeing the smile, shouted, "You've solved it? You've found the answer?" Mr. Edison replied, "Not a blamed thing works; now I can start over again." He knew hundreds of defeats before he discovered the thrill of success.

In a Christian philosophy one must make room for the inevitable experiences of life. It may not be a pleasant thought, but we must face the fact that all of us must die; there is no escape. Most of us will know the loneliness and deep sorrow that comes when we lose someone close to us. During those times, if we have a Christian faith we will know that God has not deserted us; He is near to comfort and guide us through our grief. Our Christian faith teaches us that death, as well as life, is God's plan.

The Christian is never exempted from the inevitable experiences of life. The Christian doesn't have a garment that protects him from the burdens of the day; but he has a supply of strength that enables him to be triumphant in spite of his burdens.

When Joseph Parker, an eminent British minister of another generation, was debating the enemies of Christianity on the town green, an unbeliever shouted, "What did Christ do for Stephen when he was stoned?" Dr. Parker replied, "He gave him grace to pray for those who stoned him." Stephen was killed but he was not defeated. He stands today as a symbol of what the power of God can do for those who fight the battles of life in the heat of the day.

As a small lad I was sick on several occasions. I remember them as vividly as if they were only yesterday. I was using a small child's bed which my older brother had outgrown. It was made of cast iron and the sides were up; through them I could see the dim light of a kerosene lamp. I was burning with fever, but in the shadows I could see my anxious parents. They would move occasionally to the side of my bed and place their hands on my brow. Often I would doze off to sleep and wake up to find my parents near the bed. I remember the discomfort and pain but I was never afraid as long as Mother and Father were near. Their presence was all I needed to sustain me.

We Christians do not like to endure the disappointments and sorrows of life, but when we are fortified with the knowledge that God is near, we need not be afraid. His presence will sustain us through any experience.

When Jesus saw Simon Peter and Andrew casting their net into the sea He invited them to become His disciples. He said to them, "Follow me, and I will make you fishers of men"

(MATTHEW 4:19). Jesus was constantly inviting people to follow Him. Once Jesus gave this invitation: "Whosoever will come after me, let him deny himself, and take up his cross, and follow me" (MARK 8:34). He never promised to keep us free from the temptations of life. He didn't say, "Follow me, and I will see to it that you will know joy and success." There are burdens to bear. There are Jerusalems through which we must pass, Gardens of Gethsemane in which we must linger, the rugged slopes of Calvary which we must scale. Jesus never promised the Christian an easy life but He did say, "Follow me, and I will make you. . . ." What did He mean? I believe He meant that He would make us equal to the demands of the day. Surely He meant that He would make us strong enough to bear the burdens of life.

When Lazarus died, Mary and Martha were filled with great sorrow and friends had gathered to comfort them. Actually, the presence of friends supports us during such a time, but only God can bring comfort to our hearts. Mary met Jesus outside the town and talked with Him. She knew that her sister's heart was aching with grief, so she went quickly to the house and said to Mary, "The Master is come, and calleth for thee" (JOHN 11:28).

I believe that God calls every person; He speaks to us in His persuasive way in an effort to get us to follow Him. He does not call all of us to be ministers or missionaries but He calls us; He calls us to be genuinely Christian. He calls some of us to *do* certain things, but He calls each of us to *be* a certain kind of person. What you *are* is far more important than what you *do;* that is to say, you may be a street-sweeper or a heart surgeon, but the difference that determines your destiny is not what you do, but what you are. I would rather pick up the debris left by a thoughtless humanity while walking in the footsteps of God than sleep in the bed of a king, eat from sterling silver plates, and drink from golden goblets while holding the hand of Satan.

Everyone has failed at sometime. No serious-minded person would claim that his or her life has been perfect. Our spiritual failure is reflected in war, crime, divorce, and in many other areas. The road from spiritual failure to triumphant living is not easy to travel, and we do not stumble into the Christian life by accident. It is achieved only by divine grace and diligent human effort. Let me suggest four steps that one must take in order to move from spiritual failure to triumphant living:

1. Take a look within! How long has it been since you gave some serious thought to your life? Has it been a month, a year, or perhaps never?

In taking a trip recently on some unfamiliar roads, we found it necessary to check the road map frequently; otherwise, we would have become lost. Life is like that. Each day we travel a road that is unfamiliar to us. We neet new opportunities and challenges; we face new battles and different problems. We need a spiritual road map to guide us safely through the perplexing problems of each day. Jesus said, "I am the way, the truth, and the life . . ." (JOHN 14:6). In Christ we have our best Example and Guide.

I have a friend who will tell you very readily, "I'm not a religious man," and, of course, the way he lives makes that statement totally unnecessary. However, since having a little physical trouble, he has become a regular visitor to the doctor's office. He has a complete checkup every four months. I don't quarrel with that at all; he probably needs it. One day we were talking about the important things of life and he seemed to be getting rather serious about giving his life to God. I said, "Bill, if you were half as concerned with your soul as you are with your gall bladder, you would be a much better fellow." I could tell that he didn't like what I said, but it just might lead him to see life in its true perspective.

A person ought to examine his life in the light of two important questions. First, What am I doing that I know is out of harmony with the life and teachings of Jesus? This is very much like going to a physician. A good doctor will make every effort to localize the difficulty and try to discover the cause.

Once I talked to a man who was unhappy and I asked, "Do you know why you are unhappy?" He replied, "I really can't say why." Before he left I advised him to get away from the busy rush of things and find some quiet spot where he could think. I told him to take a pencil and some paper and write down, after prayerful thought, all the things about him that he knew to be wrong. Then I advised him to come back and talk with me again. Some weeks later he called to thank me for helping him. "I did what you told me to do, and when I discovered my problem I was able, with God's help, to solve it."

Next, examine your life in the light of another question: What can I do to improve my life? Actually, this is the second thing a physician would do once he had made a diagnosis of an illness; he wants to make the patient well again. A businessman would be foolish if he didn't spend some time each week trying to determine better ways of doing his job; competition demands it.

Just think of the transformation that would take place in homes across the nation if each member of each family would consider what he or she could do in order to be a better person. Suppose a mother gave some prayerful thought to this question: "What can I do to be a better wife and mother?" Suppose a father gave some serious thought to the same question, as it applied to him? Suppose each child did the same? Do you see the potential in such self-examination?

Let me be quick to add that self-examination is not sufficient to move one from spiritual failure to triumphant living. It is only the first step. It is not enough to know what is wrong with one's life and to discover ways to improve it. Other steps are essential.

2. You must want to be a better person; then you must work toward that end. I have always wanted to play a piano. In my childhood home we had a piano and I could have taken lessons, but I had a greater desire to play with the neighborhood children. Therefore, I never learned to play the piano. You do not learn to live triumphantly by merely desiring it any more than you learn to play the piano by desiring it. To become an accomplished pianist you must spend many hours with some fine musician and at the keyboard. If you would climb to the heights of triumphant living you must spend some time with the Master. You must be willing to let Him make you a fisher of men.

Columbus spent many years trying to get someone to believe in him, and if he had not been a man of perseverance he would have deserted his dream. For eighteen long years Columbus worked untiringly amid poverty, neglect, and ridicule, trying to solicit funds for his mission. The prime of his life was spent in the struggle, but as a result he was able to set sail from Palos on August 3, 1492. It was his desire plus his determined effort that finally brought him success.

Columbus fought against heavy odds when his crew did not cooperate with him. They pleaded with him to turn back, for they had lost their faith in the venture. That did not shake Columbus' determination; he made the following entry in his diary day after day: "This day we sailed on." He did not say, "We have reached our destination."

You and I have not attained many of our goals. We are not yet the persons we had hoped to become. Some of us have fallen short of the things our loved ones have wished for us. But let us write in our spiritual diaries, "This day we sailed on, and we will continue to sail toward worthy ports if God gives us another tomorrow." There is hope for the person who sees in the distant future a spark of hope that keeps him moving toward his cherished goals. The fellow who pulls in his oars and takes down his sail cannot expect to reach the safety of the harbor. The person who loses his desire and determination will never win a worthwhile battle in life.

Robert Louis Stevenson, one of my favorite authors, was a weak, frail boy and was sick almost from the cradle to the grave. Yet Stevenson wrote to a friend, "For fourteen years I have not had one day of real health. I have wakened sick and gone to bed weary, and yet I have done my work unflinchingly." In the light of his history, the following prayer he wrote takes on fresh meaning: "We thank Thee for this place in which we dwell; for the love which unites us; for the peace that is accorded us; for the hope with which we expect the morrow; for the wealth, the work, the food and the bright skies that make our lives delightful. . . ." These words make me want to do something for humanity which will make me worthy of the privilege of life.

3. We must repent of our wrongs and accept God's forgiveness. I use the word *repent* instead of the word *confess* because the meanings of words change and often we get the wrong impression. For example, the word *confess* means an acknowledgement of our sins; it also denotes our helplessness in our sins.

We need to do more about our lives than simply confess that we are sinners; we must also seek God's forgiveness. I know people who live constantly in the awareness of their sins, but they make little or no effort to attain God's forgiveness.

The word *repent* is a stronger word which clearly implies confession. Unless one acknowledges his sins, he can never repent. Repentance has a twofold meaning: it means that one turns away from and forsakes his sins; it also means that one reaches out toward God. Genuine repentance assures one of God's forgiveness, for whenever a person forsakes his sins and turns toward God he finds the door ajar. He can always enter and find God's measureless mercy and forgiving love.

Forgiveness involves both God and man—man only to the extent that he has sins from which he needs to be saved and must be willing to forsake his sins and turn to God. The act of forgiveness depends ultimately on the divine; it is through God's mercy and love that forgiveness is possible. When man repents, this merely opens the door whereby he may experience redemption.

Man cannot redeem himself. He is capable only of the desire to be redeemed, and God must take over at this point. Norman Vincent Peale related a story told to him by the manager of a hotel in which a barbers' supply association held a convention. As a publicity stunt the barbers found a most unpromising specimen of manhood, a dirty, drunk, and ragged man. His beard was long and his hair was matted with filth. They took him to the hotel, gave him a bath, a haircut, a shave, and dressed him in a good suit, an overcoat, a hat, spats, and gave him a cane. Photographs were taken of each step and they appeared in the daily newspaper. It was a marvelous transformation, and the man didn't look like the same person. People were amazed at what the barbers could do to a person's appearance.

The hotel manager was impressed and after the convention he offered the man a job in another hotel which he operated. "Now your great opportunity is at hand. We are going to make a successful man out of you," he told him. "When will you go to work?" The man responded, "Suppose we make it tomorrow morning at eight o'clock."

The next morning the man did not appear; neither did he appear the following day, and the manager of the hotel went to the street where the barbers had found him. There he was, sprawled out on the street, dead drunk! His clothes were soiled and wrinkled.

The hotel manager remarked, "The barbers may have been able to clean him up on the outside, but you can never make anything out of a man until you also change him on the inside." And that is God's business. You may wash your skin but God must redeem your soul.

Being redeemed is a personal experience. Our great-grandparents, grandparents, and parents may have lived in the shadow of the cross, conscious of God's forgiveness and aware of His love; yet this does not assure us of a place in God's Kingdom. Bishop Arthur J. Moore told the story about Harry Denman, who came to a southern state to preach in a revival meeting. Dr. Denman had been invited to stay in a lovely home and when the thoughtful hostess showed him to the room he would occupy she remarked, "Dr. Denman, this is the room in which my grandmother prayed." Dr. Denman replied in his tender fashion, "I am not interested in where your grandmother prayed. Where do you pray?"

The crucial issue with which you and I ought to be concerned is not so much where our forefathers stood in relation to God, but where we stand. Our destiny is determined not by their goodness, but by our own. I don't mind hearing people talk about the consecration and loyalty of their relatives, but we must face the fact that we cannot get to heaven on their recommendation. Let us strive to live in such a way that our grandchildren will be able to point out our virtues as examples to others.

4. To live triumphantly we must anchor our trust in God. I see many people who seem to be indifferent to God, living as if they do not need Him. These people enjoy the warm sunshine of good health and the gentle breeze of prosperity. But in every life some shadows will fall and the night will come, and unless we have a light of faith we will stumble and fall. The mountain tops that once glistened in the bright sunshine will then stand like grotesque monsters waiting to defeat us. Faith in God is not a luxury; it is a necessity.

When I was a lad we kept a kerosene lantern at home. We never used it during the day, but when night came it provided the light we needed for doing chores. During the day we cleaned the globe, filled the lamp with oil, and kept it in good repair because we knew the night would come. The wise person will begin to develop his faith while the sun shines in order to be prepared for the dark nights that are sure to come.

The Psalmist said, ". . . for in thee do I put my trust" (16:1). He knew he was not immune to the trials and tribulations of life. He knew the dark night would come, but he proclaimed his unwavering faith in God. When the dark nights came, he knew God would guide him: ". . . my reins also instruct me in the night seasons" (v. 7). His faith in God taught him that he would never be forsaken. "Thou wilt shew me the path of life . . . ," he proclaimed (v. 11).

A passenger vessel was steaming at full speed on the St. Lawrence River. The fog was thick and some of the passengers became frightened and complained to the first mate that the captain was careless. The sailor smiled and said, "Don't be afraid. The fog lies low, but the captain is high above it and can see where we are going." There are times in life when we can't see the way ahead, but if God is leading us, let us not be afraid. He stands high on the bridge, above the fogs of earth, and He can see where we are going. Trust Him!

The road of life winds through valleys, chasms, hills, and high parts. Some of the way is smooth and easy; some is rugged and difficult. If you carry only logic with you, it will take you part of the way; but somewhere on the road of life logic will leave you stranded. You may take only knowledge, but far from heaven's portals knowledge will become weary and exhausted. You may choose to take reason, but reason's light will grow dim before the journey is over. These are all good companions but they are not sufficient. The person who spans the dark chasms of life and who scales the rugged peaks must have faith as his constant companion. Remember the words of Jesus: ". . . all things are possible to him that believeth" (MARK 9:23). The sun may shine tomorrow in your life, or the clouds may descend—but with faith in God you can be triumphant.

4

Refuse to Give Up

A YOUNG UNIVERSITY student writes, "What can you recommend for one who has been disappointed, beaten, and defeated almost constantly? The lamp of Christian faith has gone out and the future looks as dark as night." I wrote back, suggesting several things that one can do when the lamps of faith flicker and darkness covers the soul: "First, if you have abandoned the Christian faith I have no words of hope or encouragement. Outside of the truths proclaimed by the Christian faith there is little left upon which a man may hang his eternal hopes. One must begin by believing that at the very heart of this universe there is an intelligent order and that God is the Creator of life, the strength of this journey, and the goal of our pilgrimage.

"There is another road open to those who find life difficult. You can sit down with your broken dreams and complain about life." I often receive letters from people who have made this decision. They brood over what might have been and find it difficult to face what is. Somehow these people forget that God stands near to sustain them in sorrow and give them the strength to be triumphant over their deep hurts. Jesus said, "Come unto me, all ye that labour and are heavy laden, and I will give you rest" (MATTHEW 11:28). I have yet to know a man who has succeeded in this business of living and who is content to sit and brood over his broken dreams. I have known a good many people who became triumphant over what appeared to be overwhelming odds.

I received a letter from a woman who was once walking

through the sunshine of life, with joy throbbing in her heart at every step. She was a devoted and loyal member of her church. Then, without warning, tragedy struck: her only daughter was killed in an accident. Like many people, during these first moments of agony and deep hurt she cried, "Why? Why, God?" Little satisfaction is derived from such a question, and God is under no obligation to answer it. "This," she wrote, "seemed to be the end of the road. There was no tomorrow, as far as I was concerned. There was only the anguish and hurt of the present."

Suddenly this brokenhearted woman realized that all she had left were some broken dreams and some tomorrows that looked dismal and empty. She fell on her knees and asked God to give her the strength to bear her sorrow and the courage to face each tomorrow with confidence. "God brought me through those hard days," she wrote, "and I have found Him in each tomorrow."

"You could decide," I went on to advise the young student, "in spite of your disappointments, to keep going, believing that in some dark tomorrow God will speak to you and reveal His will unto you." There are many things that I do not know about God; but I know that, if I am faithful to Him, I will not walk alone. He will tap me gently on the shoulder and assure me of His presence when the night comes.

"Don't give up; life may be hard but it is never impossible—and with God's help, even you can be victorious," is advice I frequently give people. A passport to sail on a luxury liner upon smooth seas does not come with this thing we call life. Life offers us an opportunity and it places before us all the raw materials we need in order to build a useful existence; it assures us that we can be triumphant over sorrows, disappointments, and temptations. Such a life is realized only by those who refuse to give up in the face of failure and frustration.

Suppose Cyrus Field had given up! He was acclaimed the "man of the hour" for his success in laying a cable between America and Europe, but it took him over ten years to complete that task. Failure and disappointment seemed to be part of his daily diet, and the skeptics had laughed. In spite of the opposition, Cyrus Field held to his belief that a cable connecting America and Europe could be placed on the floor of the ocean. This accomplishment would speed up communications by several days. Storms at sea caused many grave problems in laying the cable; when success was within sight, the cable broke, and grappling hooks had to be lowered more than two thousand feet to recover the lost cable. Cyrus Field crossed the ocean a total of forty-one times and worked for more than a decade, but the thing we remember about him is that he finished the job.

Suppose Jesus had surrendered to His opposition and yielded to the mounting darkness that began to descend upon Him during His last few months on earth! The religious leaders of the day turned against Him; they wanted Him out of the way. Had it not been for His great popularity, the scheming leaders would have made their move weeks earlier. Jesus even faced the disappointment of betrayal: He was betrayed by one who had followed Him and been a part of His little band for almost three years; then He saw Peter, the disciple whom He trusted and with whom He had spent many hours of close fellowship, desert and deny Him. On the night He was betrayed the air was thick with hate and injustice, and evil was on the march.

The Garden of Gethsemane was a great trial for our Lord. The agony He felt cannot be described; great drops of blood came to His forehead. His disciples were asleep when He wanted their support. They might have been a source of great comfort to Him during that awful hour, but they proved to be selfish.

In spite of the darkness Jesus walked to Calvary with an unfaltering faith. He drew from a Power beyond Himself. He was, to use a phrase of an old song, ". . . leaning on the everlasting arms." He finished His task; He walked out into the darkness that surrounded Calvary and found God waiting. I don't know how dark tomorrow looks to you, but I do know that if you were to walk out in faith God would be waiting for you, ready to give you all you need in order to be faithful.

Only God knows what tomorrow will bring. The future is in His hands. We may walk in the sunshine on hilltops of laughter and joy. We may feel the gentle breeze on our cheeks and hear the birds sing. This we would like. But if this is the path we tread, let us be exceedingly cautious. It is during such times that we are likely to feel that God is not necessarily an essential part of our lives.

On the other hand, tomorrow may find us in some deep ravine where the circumstances of life have left us wounded and bleeding from hurts and sorrow. The hilltops may be hidden by bitter disappointments. Tears may flow down cheeks that once knew only joy. Saddness and a sense of frustration may fill hearts that only yesterday throbbed with gladness.

If, tomorrow, life leads us to drink the essence of sorrow and to bear heavy burdens of disappointment, how are we to react? Let us face tomorrow aware of the defeats, disappointments, and sorrows that may be ours, but let us be conscious also of the fact that God's grace is sufficient for our every need. Remember three things as we face each new day:

1. God is with us. Across these many centuries of recorded history no man has ever retreated from his duty or fallen under the load as long as he was aware of the presence of God. Once we realize that we are not alone in life, we find new courage. It is often the terrible feeling of aloneness that defeats us.

There is a wonderful story told by F. W. Boreham about an old Scotsman who, during a period of grave illness, was visited by his minister. As the minister seated himself near the bed he noticed on the opposite side another chair placed in a position that suggested another visitor had occupied it. "Well, Donald," the minister remarked, looking in the direction of the chair, "I see that I am not your first visitor." The Scotsman looked a bit surprised, and the minister pointed to the chair. "Ah!" the patient replied, "let me tell you about that chair. Some years ago I had great difficulty staying awake when I prayed. Often I would be so weary that I would fall asleep on my knees while praying. If I managed to stay awake I frequently found it hard to keep my thoughts from wandering. I spoke to the minister and he advised me not to worry about kneeling down. 'Just sit down,' he suggested, 'and put a chair opposite you. Imagine that Jesus is in it, and talk to Him as you would to a friend.' "

The old man added, "I have been doing that ever since, and that is why the chair is there."

A few days later the daughter of the old Scot drove to the minister's home and asked to see him. She was taken to the study and with great emotion she told the minister that her father had died during the night. "I had no idea death could be so near," she said. "I had just gone to lie down for an hour or two. He seemed to be sleeping so comfortably. And when I went back, he was dead. He hadn't moved since I saw him before, except that his hand was out on the empty chair at the side of his bed." The presence of God is a mighty comforting thing as we journey through life.

2. Let us forget our weakness and remember God's strength. The Psalmist said, "My help cometh from the Lord . . ." (121:2). No wonder we experience so much despair and frustration—we have tried to reduce God to little more than humanity and to elevate man to some form of divinity. I am not implying that God moves when we snap our fingers, but I am pointing out that beyond human wisdom and brawn there is divine help. To forget this truth spells disaster.

God expects us to do our part, and to ask Him to do what we can do for ourselves is the essence of spiritual crudeness. He endowed humanity with the tools of reason, wisdom, and strength, but the gifts of God carry with them certain obligations. On the other hand, to stand alone when human wisdom and strength are exhausted, and to refuse to ask for God's help, is the height of egotistical stupidity.

A few months ago our oldest son, who is little more than four years old, came to the study with grimy hands and sweaty brow. "Daddy," he exclaimed, "I want you to come and move a big rock for me." After a short pause, he said, impatiently, "Daddy, I need you to help me!"

"Sit down for a minute, and let's talk," I suggested. "Before I go, I want to know if you have tried to move the stone."

With the skill of a trained psychologist, he remarked, "Yes, I have tried to move it, and I am not strong enough. But daddies are big and strong and they can do anything."

There was some good theology wrapped up in his statement. It reflected the fact that my son had done his best and still had failed; his best was not good enough. It also reflected the fact that he knew where he could get the help he needed. When his best efforts failed, he refused to give up in defeat.

Let's transfer these thoughts to our relationship with God. In every life there are some rocks that need to be moved. Old habits bind us to evil ways. We need more patience and understanding. We need to take another step toward a deeper consecration to God. The lamp of faith flickers and the soot of doubt keeps us from seeing God's will for our lives. The flaming coals of love are fading into cold gray ashes.

Have we done our best to live the Christian life? And in spite of our best efforts, do we face defeat and despair? If we have come to the end of human strength, let us turn to Someone stronger and wiser. Let us remember that the end of human effort is merely the beginning of God's help. When we turn in faith and surrender our weaknesses to God and say with the Psalmist, "My help cometh from the Lord," we will discover that He can supply all our needs.

3. Finally, keep in mind that others have endured the sorrows and defeats we are now experiencing. Misery fails to find much comfort in company, yet when we walk through the dark parts of life we sometimes feel that we are in a jungle through which no other living soul has ever passed. The path through the jungle of sorrow, defeat, and disappointment has been beaten smooth by the bleeding feet of other suffering souls. The fact we need to remember is that they have been sustained, and I am certain that God will sustain us too as we walk this way. We can hear God whisper to us, as others have heard Him whisper, "My grace is sufficient for thee . . ." (II CORINTHIANS 12:9).

5

You Can Meet
and Master Your Problems

EVERY PERSON ON the sea of life must face the high waves, strong winds, and dark nights. Man can never reach his destiny by throwing out his anchor in the safety of some placid harbor. Before our journey ends we shall know what it is like to be disappointed and hurt; we shall know the empty feeling that accompanies broken dreams, crushed hopes, and lonely grief.

Jesus talked about persecutions, sufferings, scattered sheep, and a cross. He looked men in the face and without hiding the demands of discipleship said, "If any man will come after me, let him deny himself, and take up his cross daily, and follow me" (LUKE 9:23). Paul talked about the soldier's equipment in his Letter to the Ephesians: "Put on the whole armour of God, that ye may be able to stand against the wiles of the devil" (6:11). A good soldier must be prepared for the battles of life, and Paul urged the Ephesians to wear the breastplate of righteousness, to gird their loins with truth, and to wear on their feet the gospel of peace. He also urged them not to forget the shield of faith, the helmet of salvation, and the sword of the spirit. Man's greatest challenge is not to reach the moon or conquer outer space, but to conquer himself and live according to the teachings of Jesus Christ.

All through the New Testament we find Jesus desperately trying to prepare men for the storms of life. We find here and there a compass to guide us and a lighthouse on the rough sea to steer us away from the hidden rocks that could dash us to pieces. You and I cannot know what the future will bring us, but somewhere on the distant horizon we will know sorrow. There is no way around it, but there is a way through it. Yes, God will guide us. Minnie Louise Haskins expressed this faith in her famous words: "And I said to the man who stood at the gate to the year: 'Give me a light that I may tread safely into the unknown.' And he replied: 'Go out into the darkness and put your hand into the hand of God. That shall be to you better than light and safer than a known way.'"

How do we go about finding the power to meet and master life? If I wanted to excel in golf I would find the greatest golf player and study his swing and watch him play. He would be my example. If I wanted to become a skilled surgeon I would attend the best medical school and seek out the greatest surgeon and watch him work and study his methods. If we are really interested in mastering life we must study the life of Jesus Christ and make Him our Example. He faced temptations with fortitude; He met hostility with love; He stood alone with an unwavering confidence when His disciples forsook Him; He went to the Garden of Gethsemane armed with an unshakable hope; He stood with an unfaltering faith before the vicious court that tried Him; He walked with a steady step to Calvary, believing that out of the hate, injustice, and suffering of that tragic event God would be glorified and the enemy would be defeated.

If we are to meet and master the problems that plague us, we must be like Jesus. "That is easy to prescribe," you may say, "but impossible to achieve." I must admit that I do not know any person whose life possesses the same depth of wisdom, height of love, width of concern, and breadth of purpose so clearly manifested in the life of Jesus. We find it hard to love our neighbors, to say nothing of our enemies. We have not learned to pray with the same enthusiasm for those who would persecute us as we do for those we love. It is very difficult to walk the second mile, and most of us have not grown enough spiritually to turn the other cheek.

Many of us would admit that we could, with a little effort, be more like Jesus than we are now. We could exercise a little more patience; we could refuse to speak when what we have to say would hurt another. Let us pray for the understanding that we so desperately need in order to be more tolerant where tolerance is God's will. Let us ask God to make us more sensitive to the feelings of others. The truth is, most of us are not making any effort to live as our Lord lived. We want His poise and peace without His discipline and dedication. We would like to have His power and strength without sharing either the responsibility of His commitment or the demands of His loyalty.

Little wonder we are buried in a sea of perplexing problems. Too many of us want the assurance and peace that only God can give, but we want them gift-wrapped in the glittering paper our modern society likes and tied with the ribbons of respectability. This cannot be achieved. Jesus said, "No man can serve two masters: for either he will hate the one, and love the other; or else he will hold to the one, and despise the other. Ye cannot serve God and mammon" (MATTHEW 6:24).

If you and I are to meet and master the problems of life we must be transformed from the evils that surround us, not conformed to them. That was our Lord's secret; that was Paul's secret—and it must be ours.

Some people want a philosophy that affirms the way they live. Isn't it strange how we manage to justify our sins and rationalize our wrongs! The man who becomes dishonest in his business dealings justifies it on the basis of competition. The family heading for the lake on Sunday convince themselves that everybody has the right to a little recreation. The student who cheats on the examination soothes his conscience by whispering to himself, "There's really nothing wrong in doing this." The woman who drinks liquor every day eases her guilt by saying, "What harm could this possibly do? I can't hurt anyone but myself. I am the only one involved." She forgets that those who love her will be hurt, and her friends and neighbors are involved because of her influence. Whether or not she realizes it, God is involved.

The man who forgets his marriage vows and becomes unfaithful to his wife can think of a hundred reasons why he is entitled to engage in the sin of infidelity. The automobile salesman who sells a car to a customer for more than he knows it is worth might soothe his conscience by complimenting himself on being a clever salesman. The young person who engages in immoral acts might rationalize the sin by saying, "It's the one sure way of achieving popularity." We forget that God does not judge us by what is accepted or by what others are doing. He will judge us by what He expects us to accomplish in life.

A person can never have the power to meet and master life if he continually covers his sins, rationalizes his evil behavior, and blames someone else for the stains on his soul. We can never be free from guilt until we are willing to face ourselves. The Prodigal Son looked at his life and said, "Father, I have sinned against heaven, and before thee, And am no more worthy to be called thy son: make me as one of thy hired servants" (LUKE 15:18-19). Not until a man sees himself as a sinner, standing in need of God's forgiveness, and not until he commits himself to God, will he be able to meet and master life.

Some people want to belong to a church in which their sins are rarely discussed. They seem delighted when the minister talks about the sins or virtues of David, and they don't mind hearing about the fortitude and faith of Job. They will listen to sermons about the cross and the resurrection, but they are not the least bit interested in hearing about their own sins.

I think a sermon ought to do at least two things. First, it ought to make people aware that they have sinned; no person ought to leave church on Sunday without seeing the sins of his soul. Second, a sermon ought to point the lost sheep toward the safety of the fold; not only must the pulpit be proficient in pointing out the evils that plague us, but it must also point to the Saviour who forgives and saves us. Our plight, no matter how bleak, is never hopeless. God is still doing business and He is eager to forgive us.

In Ian Maclaren's book *Beside the Bonnie Brier Bush*, Lachlan Campbell was very critical of the minister's sermons, especially if he did not preach to suit his own brand of theology. When John Carmichael came to be the minister of the little church, Campbell at first held back his cutting criticism. Then, soon after his arrival, the minister preached a sermon which, in the judgment of Campbell, was very poor. Others complimented the young minister but Lachlan Campbell went to his study and waited until the minister came. Without other greeting, Campbell said, "Was that what you call a sermon?" The young minister was so full of joy that he did not catch the tone of the voice in which his critic spoke. He replied, "It was hardly a sermon, nor a lecture. You might call it a meditation." Campbell retorted with stinging words: "I will be calling it an essay," he said, "without one bite of grass for starving sheep."

"What was wrong?" the anxious minister asked. "There was nothing right," Campbell replied. "I did not hear about sin and repentance and the work of Christ." Every sermon ought to feed the sheep. We must give people direction in finding forgiveness and living the abundant life.

The church, for some people, is little more than a social club filled with nice folks who make lovely friends. For them, it is the proper thing to be seen in church, and if you are temperate in your sins no one should scold you or frown upon you. The Christian church would be dead within a decade if all our people felt this way about it. But others know it as a place where they come face to face with God. Here they have found forgiveness of their sins. Here God has renewed their hopes and refreshed their energies. Here they have found the courage to face life with confidence and the strength to bear their burdens, knowing that God is good and wise. The church is more than a resting place; it must remain an emergency room where the wounds of the soul are cleansed and cured. It must stand as a point of departure from which the soldiers of the Master march out into a hostile world, seeking to save the lost.

Jesus had a stalwart faith and a spiritual fortitude that made Him the Master of life. He endured more hostility, suffering, and hardship in His thirty-three years than we do even if we live three score years and ten. He was tempted to a greater degree than you and I are tempted. His disappointments brought more pain to His heart than our disappointments bring to us. He suffered far more than you and I will suffer. Yet He was triumphant; in every case Christ was the Victor.

"I know Christ was perfect," someone remarked, "but tell me how I can live in this twentieth century and master life. I want to be triumphant but it looks like an impossible achievement." Jesus assured His disciples that He would win the battles of life: ". . . be of good cheer; I have overcome the world" (JOHN 16:33). As we watch Him in the Garden, linger with Him at Calvary, and listen to Him after the resurrection, we know that His words were more than echoes from a hopeful heart. He really did master life and He conquered the enemies of goodness.

Jesus said, "Follow me, and I will make you fishers of men" (MATTHEW 4:19). Now, Jesus did not call the disciples to perform an impossible task. God never demands that we do the impossible. We can follow Him, and there are times when we follow from afar. We do not always walk with our hand in His, but that is not an impossibility. We can be His disciples and be triumphant over the enemies of peaceful living. Look again at the life of Jesus. Study His habits and you can discover His secret. Let me suggest four things that Jesus did regularly.

1. Jesus was a student of Scripture. You cannot spend time each day reading the Bible prayerfully and diligently without catching a glimpse of the greatness of God. You will be challenged on every page to live a better life.

Jesus often quoted Scriptures. The disciples said, "Did not our heart burn within us, while he talked with us by the way, and while he opened to us the scriptures?" (LUKE 24:32). He explained the Scriptures to the disciples as they sat enthralled in His Presence.

You will find in the Bible all you need to know in order to be saved from your sins. It will not tell you everything you may want to know about God, but it will teach you all you need to know in order to reach your destiny. It offers a spark of hope for those who are ready to give up in the heat of the day. It gives comfort to those who feel the crushing hammer of sorrow. It offers strength to those whose burdens seem more than they can bear. It assures those who walk in the shadows of loneliness that they are not alone. It whispers words of cheer into the hearts of those who feel that no one really cares about them. It is a guide for those who have lost their sense of values in the jungle of life. It offers cool water to parched lips and food for hungry hearts. When life is difficult the Bible offers courage and assures us that with God's help we can be triumphant. When we lose one we love and our hearts are full of grief, the Bible tells us about the warm lights that glow forever in the Father's house. It tells us about God's concern for us and speaks of the majesty of the King.

In the pages of the Bible we are challenged to give the best we have to God. The Scriptures remind us that no life is hopelessly lost; they proclaim the best news that human ears can hear and human hearts can feel. We are reminded again and again of the unceasing love, the unfaltering care, and the gentle mercies that follow us down the corridors of time. The Bible tells us of the gentle Galilean who urges us tenderly and compassionately to surrender ourselves to God.

Dr. Daniel Marsh, once president of Boston University, told of an incident that took place during the reign of Queen Victoria. A prince from India sent the queen a letter inquiring about the secret of England's glory. In reply to this request the queen sent the prince a Bible and on the flyleaf wrote, "This book is the secret of England's glory." Dr. Marsh observed, "The same is more strikingly true of America. The early discoveries and explorations of this continent were made for the most part by men whose dominating motive was the dissemination of the religion of the Bible."

Voltaire is reputed to have said that within one hundred years the Bible would be an outmoded and forgotten Book, to be found only in museums. When the hundred years had passed, Voltaire's house was owned and used by the Geneva Bible Society, and some time ago ninety-two volumes of his own work were reputed to have been sold for only two dollars.

Jesus read the Scriptures with diligence, and you and I must read them if we want to master the problems of life.

2. Jesus attended divine worship, regularly. "And he came to Nazareth, where he had been brought up: and, as his custom was, he went into the synagogue on the sabbath day . . ." (LUKE 4:16). It was there Jesus found new hope and His relationship with God was strengthened.

The late Archbishop William Temple, in *The Hope of a New World*, wrote "This world can be saved from political chaos and collapse by one thing only and that is worship. For to worship is to quicken the conscience by the Holiness of God, to feed the mind with the truth of God, to purge the imagination by the beauty of God, to open up the heart to the love of God, to devote the will to the purpose of God."

A psychiatrist paid me a high compliment some years ago when one of his patients came to see me and told me that she had been in my congregation for several months. "I came here," she said, "on the advice of my doctor. He asked me to come to this church because you preach a gospel of hope and he said that was what I needed." Any true worship service will offer a spark of hope to those who are sensitive to God's voice.

Those who worship God regularly will make every effort to become the kind of persons God wants them to be. I firmly believe that a man who attends church every Sunday for a period of several months will either decide to do all he can to bring his life into harmony with God's will or else he will quit the church altogether.

The American humorist Artemus Ward said, "If you will show me a place where there are no houses of worship and where men do not pray, I will show you a place where people are slipshod and dirty, where gates are off their hinges, where old hats are stuffed in broken windows." Worship helps us to see our own sins and assures us that God will forgive them.

3. Jesus prayed frequently. You may be sure that a part of our Lord's secret in facing life so confidently can be found in His prayer life. Frequently in the Scriptures we read statements referring to Jesus' prayer life: ". . . and [He] went up into a mountain to pray" (LUKE 9:28).

The disciples were so captured by the power that Jesus received through His prayers that they asked Him, "Lord, teach us to pray . . ." (LUKE 11:1). Prayer, for Jesus, was a period of communion with God; He was able to find, through His prayers, the strength He needed and the guidance He wanted. His moments of prayer were not efforts on His part to get God to do things His way; rather it was the desire of Jesus to understand perfectly the will of God for His own life. You and I pray best when we come to God, not demanding that God do certain things for us, but asking, "God, what do You want me to do now?"

Prayer is an experience no person can afford to miss. I do

not see how it is possible to meet and master the difficult problems of life without making use of this high privilege of communion with God. If you want to master the little frets and cares that often rob you of radiance, turn aside and pray. Ask God to grant you peace and help you to be victorious. Jesus said, "If ye shall ask any thing in my name, I will do it" (JOHN 14:14). Many of us live in spiritual poverty because we fail to seek the help of God.

4. Jesus ministered to others. Once He said, "For even the Son of man came not to be ministered unto, but to minister, and to give his life a ransom for many" (MARK 10:45). The most satisfying things I have ever done in life are not the things I have done for myself, but the deeds I have performed for others.

Jesus Christ spent His time walking the dusty streets of Jerusalem, and up and down the shores of Galilee, as the Servant of all men. He restored the sight of blind men; he cleansed the lepers' spots; He made the lame to walk and put fresh hope in the lives of those who were despondent; He took dirty souls from the dungeon of guilt and cleansed them and set them free; He thought only of others, never of Himself. Wherever you found Jesus you found Him at work binding up the wounds of the soul and soothing fevered brows.

His command is, "Follow Me." Herein lies part of the secret of our Master's success. When we learn to study the Scriptures as diligently as He studied them, to worship as sincerely as He worshiped; to pray as unselfishly as He prayed, and to serve as fully as He served—then we can master life.

The things Jesus did reflected what He was. Jesus was committed to do His Father's will: He said, "My meat is to do the will of him that sent me, and to finish his work" (JOHN 4:34). Our Lord's faith was unwavering: when the shadow of the cross was evident Jesus said, ". . . not my will, but thine, be done" (LUKE 22:42). His purpose was steadfast; above all, Jesus wanted to remain the Son in whom His Father would be well pleased: ". . . he stedfastly set his face to go to Jerusalem" (LUKE 9:51). A cross awaited Him in Jerusalem, but Jesus was convinced that that was His divine purpose, and He would not flinch from doing what His Father wanted Him to do.

Jesus was and is a Shepherd of the sheep and a Light in the darkness. In *Beside the Bonnie Brier Bush*, Lachlan Campbell is a very religious but an exceedingly strict man. His wife had died and left him to bring up their daughter Flora, but Flora did not understand her father and ran away from home to London. At a meeting of the Session, Lachlan said he had a case of discipline to present and requested that the Session do their duty. He began by saying, "It is known to me that a member of this church has left home and gone into the far country. She will never be seen again in this parish. I move that she be cut off the roll, and her name is"—here his voice broke, but he quickly recovered his poise—"her name is Flora Campbell."

The Session was shocked and Burnbrae was the first to speak. "This is a terrible calamity that has befallen our brother. . . . None of us want to know what has happened or where she has gone, and not a word of this will cross our lips. . . . It is not the way of this Session to cut off any member of the flock at a stroke, and we'll not begin with Flora Campbell. . . . I move, Moderator, that her case be left to her father and yourself, and our neighbor may depend on it that Flora's name and his own will be mentioned in our prayers. . . ."

The minister took Lachlan's arm and led him to the manse. "Tell me about it," he said. Lachlan reached into his pocket and pulled out the letter his daughter had left. She told him that she was leaving and that she would never be worthy to come back home. She begged her father to forgive her.

Marget Howe, a saintly member of the church, went to see Lachlan about his problem. She told Lachlan that he had been too hard on his daughter. "Would to God that she was lying in the church yard," Lachlan said, "but I will not speak of her. She is nothing to me this day. See, I will show you what I have done." He opened the Bible and showed her where Flora's name had been scratched through with black ink. The ink was smeared as if it had been mingled with tears. Suddenly Lachlan began to pray, "God be merciful to me a sinner."

Eventually Marget Howe wrote a letter to Flora for Lachlan. She began: "You know that I was always your friend and I am writing to say that your father loves you more than ever. Come back. . . . Start the very minute you receive this letter; your father bids you come."

Lachlan cleaned and trimmed the lamp that was kept for company and placed it in the window. "It is dark," he said, "and Flora will be coming and she must know that her father will be waiting for her." The lamp remained in the window every night until Flora returned and its light could be seen down the steep path that led to her home, "like the Divine Love from the open door of our Father's House."

Let us not forget that the lights of the Father's house are burning brightly and we have the open invitation to come back from the far country and live with Him. If your sins have not been forgiven, start this very minute. Come back to the Father who loves you more than ever.

6

I Know

God Cares for You

VOLUMES HAVE BEEN written about Christ. Since His birth in the stable at Bethlehem He has marched across twenty centuries. There are many things we know about Christ. He is gentle, kind, and thoughtful; He is forgiving, full of compassion. His concern covers all men; His love and mercy reaches into the hearts of the lonely, the defeated, and the diseased. He knows the music that leaps from the human heart—our lips may say one thing but often our hearts say another. Jesus is sensitive to the drums of the heart which beat out a slow rhythm of hurt, sorrow, and disappointment. He hears the bugles crying out from the depths of souls for strength, hope, a light of faith, and pardon. In spite of all we know about the Galilean, He remains the unfathomable Man of creation.

I become disturbed when small minds try to discredit the work of Jesus by offering theories of logic to explain the miracles He performed, or by refusing to believe that He performed any miracles. Across the years men have tried to pick away His majesty and strip Him of His divinity, but if you whittle Christ down to the size of human logic and give Him only human wisdom and strength, then I cannot believe in Him as Saviour. If Christ did not perform miracles, then He was a liar. Unless I can believe in His power to do more than you and I can do, then I must conclude that He deceived us and was the biggest impostor in history. Actually, those who have spent their efforts cutting away His divine glory can never change the nature of Christ; they merely dwarf their own faith.

It must have been early afternoon when Jesus received a request from Jairus, a member of the synagogue, to heal his little girl. When news spread quickly that Jesus was on His way to perform a miracle, a crowd followed Him toward the home of Jairus. The crowd was excited. Many were pushing in an effort to catch a glimpse of the Master's face. On the fringe of the crowd, men argued. There was hope in Jairus' heart, yet opinion among the crowd was divided. Some believed that Jesus could make the little girl well; some doubted and were frank to suggest that He would end in utter failure; others were simply curious, not knowing what they believed. No one wanted to miss the event.

In that crowd was a woman whose face was drawn with pain and whose steps reflected the acute suffering she had endured. She had been sick for twelve long years. She probably had a bleeding cancer or some form of pernicious hemorrhage, and she appeared to be a hopeless case.

Who was the woman? No one really knows. I think it is significant that her name is unknown. She was not a person of note, she had no claim to greatness, she could not attract much attention. She stands as a symbol of the countless multitudes found in our nursing homes and hospitals today. Some of them have become almost nameless, forgotten by family and friends. Day after day they are confined to beds in tiny rooms where they lie, waiting for death to free them from the limitations of earthly existence. There is great comfort in the knowledge that though the ailing woman who waited with the crowd was not named, she was not forgotten by Christ.

The woman apparently possessed tremendous fortitude. She loved life and had done everything possible to get well. I have an idea the sufferer was probably in her middle fifties—perhaps she had grandchildren who, instead of bringing her joy, and because of her condition, made her nervous.

I once talked to a man who had been sick for a long time. After weeks of staying in bed and spending sleepless nights, he remembered with a deep sense of gratitude the simple things of life: "How wonderful it would be to get up in the morning, wash my face, eat breakfast, and take a little walk in the backyard." The woman in the crowd also longed to be well again so she could enjoy her family and live a full life.

She had spent her life savings going from one physician to another, but she had grown worse. The Bible states that the invalid ". . . had suffered many things of many physicians, and had spent all that she had, and was nothing bettered, but rather grew worse" (MARK 5:26). She might have given up in despair. Her attitude easily could have been, "What's the use! Everything has failed! I'll just give up!"

This woman is a symbol of the host of people who have tried everything in life, trying to discover spiritual healing, only to be forced to admit that everything has ended in defeat. But in spite of her failures she had kept hope alive. Suppose, after ten years of sickness, she had given up? What a pity! She never would have known good health because she would not have seen the Master.

I remember a wonderful woman who was sick for many months. During the last weeks of her illness she had great difficulty in talking, and her pain was almost unbearable. Anxious loved ones were eager for the end to come and spare her such great agony. In the final chapter of her life on earth she taught doctors, nurses, friends, and loved ones a marvelous lesson, for no one who saw her struggle and die could ever doubt the adequacy of the Christian faith. A few days before God called her home she whispered, "I don't understand why I must suffer, but I know God is with me and He will never forsake me."

I could feel the breath of the guardian angels in that room. I left, saying to myself, "That is the kind of faith Jesus expressed in the Garden of Gethsemane when He prayed, '. . . nevertheless not my will, but thine, be done' (LUKE 22:42). That's the same faith our Lord expressed on the cross when He prayed, 'Father, into thy hands I commend my spirit . . .' (LUKE 23:46). That is the faith Stephen expressed when he prayed, 'Lord, lay not this sin to their charge' (ACTS 7:60). That is the faith Job reflected when he said, 'Though he slay me, yet will I trust in him . . .' (JOB 13:15). That is the kind of faith that will be triumphant in any situation." Such faith is not bound by what is logical or reasonable; it has complete trust in the goodness and wisdom of God. That kind of faith never fails; rather it always carries us to the heights of triumphant living.

Some say the ailing woman came to Jesus because He was a sort of "last court of appeals." The facts substantiate this belief: she had tried everything other than faith in God. However, let us not be harsh in our judgments, because Jesus had been preaching only a few months and the woman had been sick for twelve years; perhaps that was the first time she had heard of Jesus. The truth remains that Jesus is our only hope.

If anyone deserves criticism for failing to find spiritual healing, it is our generation. Most of us have been brought up in homes where the name of Jesus was not only honored but worshiped. We teach our children the stories of Jesus. His name is flashed across the airwaves and printed in our magazines and newspapers. We have the benefit of almost two thousand years of testimony about Christ. Still, many of us are looking for peace of mind in the comforts and pleasures of a material world. Although we know about Jesus, many of us have failed to give Him a chance in our lives.

I have often wondered who told that woman about Jesus. Was it a friend who brought the news to her? Perhaps it was a loved one! The only thing that matters is that someone talked to her about Jesus. Maybe the conversation went something like this: "Jesus is coming this way, and you know what others are saying about Him! Some have been healed by His touch. Blind men have been healed—they have discarded their sticks! Jesus even healed the lepers. Why not try Jesus?" How long has it been since you invited someone to "try Jesus"?

People often ask me, "What can I do for the church?" The question ought to be changed a little and we ought to ask, "What can I do for God?" Well, God has done many things for us but there is at least one thing we can do to express our gratitude to Him. We can act as if we know and love Him. We can tell others, by the way we live, that we are His disciples. How long has it been since you told someone—perhaps verbally, or maybe by your actions—that in God there is hope? The greatest weakness of the Christian church in this generation is that those of us who wave the flag of the church and wear her uniform do not act like Christ.

Often our devotion is lagging. If we were to measure the meaning of our Christianity by our attendance at church, we would conclude that it doesn't mean very much to some of us. A college student who attends classes only when the weather is pleasant, or when he doesn't have a guest on campus, or when there isn't a sports spectacular in town, will fail. The soldier who goes to drill and rifle practice only when he wants to do so will never be prepared for battle. We often neglect God and His church and then wonder why we aren't strong enough to face the battles of life when they crowd in upon us.

If we were to measure the meaning of our Christianity by the way we show our concern and compassion for others, it would be evident that our faith does not mean very much to us. Some of us live as if we care little for our own souls, and have even less concern for those around us. The man who heads for the lake instead of the sanctuary on Sunday has a distorted sense of values. He may justify his action to himself, but I have an idea he will have a difficult time justifying it to God.

If we were to measure the meaning of our Christianity by the amount we give to the church, we would be forced to conclude that the church doesn't mean much to some of us. Too many people give the church what is left after all other needs and desires have been met. I have heard people say, "I'll give to the church when I feel like it," or "I want to give out of desire." How many of us pay our taxes simply because we want to? Do we pay our bills because we want to?

Many of us wear the uniform of the Christian church, but we don't act like disciplined soldiers of the cross. The greatest compliment we can pay God is to act like the Christ whose name we bear.

The sick woman didn't make excuses. She didn't say, "Oh, there is such a multitude that I couldn't even get near Him. I'll wait for a more convenient time—perhaps He will pass this way again. Then I'll make my move." That weak, frail woman moved into the crowd and managed to get near Jesus. No one paid any attention to her as she moved close to the Master. It was a daring venture for her, but when she caught a glimpse of

Him she knew He would be considerate and gentle. Her faith grew and she said to herself, "If I may touch but his clothes, I shall be whole" (MARK 5:28).

Can you imagine the excitement of that woman? She didn't ask for an interview; she didn't even feel it was necessary for Christ to know she was there. Her faith was so strong that she believed that touching the hem of His garment would heal her of her disease.

As soon as the confident woman touched Jesus, she knew she was healed. There was no magic in the Master's clothes; the power was found in the woman's faith. Jesus knew that "virtue had gone out of him," and He turned around and asked, "Who touched my clothes?" (MARK 5:30). The disciples answered, in effect, "Look at the multitude! How do You expect us to know who touched You?"

Jesus looked into the woman's eyes and she began to tremble and "fell down before him, and told him all the truth" (MARK 5:33). The poor woman found Someone who really cared for her. For a few moments Jesus focused His attention upon the needs of a woman whose name has been lost to history. He did not resent the fact that she touched the hem of His garment, and there was no scorn or ridicule in His voice as He spoke to her. Hers was a faith unclouded by intellectual doubts. Jesus said, with tenderness and compassion, "Daughter, thy faith hath made thee whole; go in peace, and be whole of they plague" (MARK 5:34).

Our faith is often hampered by what is logical, or limited by what appears reasonable. But that woman believed that Jesus could do for her what others had failed to do; she believed that the Galilean could do for her what He had done for others. The Master did not disappoint her. One line of a song we sing reveals her faith:

> It is no secret what God can do,
> What He's done for others, He'll do for you.

The disciples thought it was unreasonable that Jesus could feel the touch of one person in a multitude. Even today, there are many who think it absurd that God could be concerned with just one person. Yet all through the Bible we read of the worth of a single person, and Jesus said, "For what shall it profit a man, if he shall gain the whole world, and lose his own soul?" (MARK 8:36). The Psalmist, when considering the glory and greatness of the universe, asked, "What is man, that thou art mindful of him?" (8:4).

There are those who have lost sight of a personal God who cares for the individual. Once Jesus described how God clothes the grass of the field and provides food for the fowls of the air. He pointed out that the birds do not sow, neither do they reap; ". . . yet your heavenly Father feedeth them" (MATTHEW 6:26). Then Jesus explained how much more God is willing to do for those who are made in His image. We live constantly under the care of a loving God whose wisdom is unquestionable and whose mercy is unfathomable. Jesus was on His way to heal a sick girl and He could have said to the woman, "I'm busy now. I will see you tomorrow." Of course, that is not His nature. A suffering woman had a need and the Master was glad to stop and minister to her.

Jesus spoke to the multitudes, but He ministered to individuals. He had compassion on another woman whose body was bent with pain; she could not walk and had been sick for eighteen years. "And he laid his hands on her: and immediately she was made straight, and glorified God" (LUKE 13:13). He raised the widow's son; He saw the grieved mother following the casket of her only son and He had mercy on the brokenhearted woman and told her not to weep. Then He said, "Young man, I say unto thee, Arise. And he that was dead sat up, and began to speak" (LUKE 7:14-15). As He entered Jericho, Jesus ministered to the blind beggar and restored his sight.

Don't ever say, "God doesn't love or care for me." There are those who have convinced themselves that God doesn't care about them, or that God is no longer interested in them, or that they do not really count because they are only tiny individuals in God's vast creation. But the touch of an unknown woman caused Jesus to stop, "And he looked round about to see her . . ." (MARK 5:32).

The Bible tells us that God cares. Jesus reflects God's interest in humanity and the church proclaims His divine concern and love. How much does God care? That is truly a significant question. It is a question that can never be answered fully in this life, but some day, if we are faithful to God, we will know the answer in its entirety. God cares about us enough to send His Son into an evil and hostile world to save us from our sins. You can't begin to understand God's interest in you until you stand near Calvary and watch as Jesus climbs those rugged slopes and is nailed to a cross. Then you begin to feel, in some small measure, God's love for all of humanity.

The power to cleanse the soul does not come by standing in the crowd and observing. It comes by *touching* the Master. Many of us observe from the church pew; we come close to the Master but we never really touch Him. Many of us want to be good but we do not want to be Christian. We want to stay in sight of Jesus but we are not willing to touch Him.

We desperately need to touch the Master. We have sins that need to be forgiven, little jealousies that ought to be removed, and ugly sores of grudges that need the healing touch of the Master's hand. Can we pray for those who are thoughtless and treat us unjustly? Can we forgive those who have hurt us? Can we swallow our pride and confess to others that we have been wrong and thereby mend a broken relationship? Unless we walk near enough to touch the Master, and unless we reach out our hands in faith to touch Him, we can never have the grace to forgive our enemies, to pray for those who have hurt us, and to work diligently toward mending broken relationships.

Some who read these lines may need healing of body or mind or spirit. Others may need divine guidance for a problem. Still others may need forgiveness. Then there are those who need strength to bear the burdens of the day. All of us need to touch the Master because we are never self-sufficient, and most of us would freely admit that. But the big question is, *How can I touch the Master?* There are several ways:

1. We must concede that although God does not walk the earth today in the form of human flesh, we know that His presence is near. God is not only the force behind this universe but His presence is as real as the automobiles in which we ride, the ground upon which we walk, and the houses in which we

live. We touch Him with the hand of prayer extended on the arm of faith. Go and tell God about your problems. Talk to Him as you would to your best friend.

2. Believe that God hears you. It is completely beyond my comprehension to understand how God's attention is focused in my direction when I go to Him in prayer, yet I believe it is possible. We get individual attention from God. He has many sheep, but the Bible tells us that He knows each one by name.

3. Listen for God to speak to you. God always answers prayer; perhaps the answer is not the one we seek, but His answer will be best. There are times when we do not understand God's answer to prayer, but we must trust Him.

You can touch God. He is here—not in flesh and flowing robes, but in Spirit. Be as daring in your faith as the poor, nameless woman who wanted to touch only the hem of Jesus' garment, and a miracle can be performed in your life. When we touch Him He will heal us or give us grace to stand. When we touch the Master we will have victory over our trials and troubles or victory in them.

Once a woman of great faith told me the secret of her ability to walk through sorrow and sickness. She said, "I just hold out my hand when the way is dark, and God always takes it." If you are stumbling through some dark valley, why not hold out your hand in faith? God will take it and lead you safely through.

7

Give God a Chance

THE SALE OF pills advertised to relieve tension and promote relaxation broke all records last year. Doctors' waiting rooms are crowded with worried and anxious people. It sometimes takes several weeks to get an appointment with a psychiatrist. Professional counselors of all types are reporting a booming business. Ours is truly a restless generation.

Why are we burdened with fear and filled with anxiety? We have more automobiles, television sets, bathtubs, deep freezers, and dishwashers than ever before. The average American has more money, a better home, nicer clothes, and more leisure time than he has ever enjoyed. We have more centers of culture, universities, and places of recreation than ever before. In spite of all this, many of us feel that we are moving aimlessly through life, and our goals never come into sharp focus.

We should have learned by now that happiness is not found in material possessions. God created man for a destiny that reaches beyond an easy existence, and if we are to discover genuine peace we must find it in God. To ignore Him is chaos. It matters not how respectable we may be, or how high our friends may hold us in their esteem—unless we take God by the hand, all the glitter in the world leaves the human soul numb and desolate. We must learn to break through the shallow crust of materialism if we are to find life's true purpose.

In my early ministry I had an occasion to talk to a man on his deathbed. He came from a poverty-stricken family, and his major goal in life had been to make money. During his productive years, he managed to amass a fortune but he didn't realize how temporary the material things of life are until he became aware of the fact that his life was quickly ebbing away. "I've been a very foolish man," he said. "I have deceived myself. I believed that money was the chief end of life. Now, after a lifetime of making money, I have discovered that wealth is reduced to nothing in the presence of death. If I had the opportunity to live my life over, I would spend it for God." There is absolutely no substitute for the sure knowledge that God holds us by the hand, and when we are called to walk through the valley of death we shall fear no evil because God will guide us.

Jesus said, ". . . lay up for yourselves treasures in heaven, where neither moth nor rust doth corrupt, and where thieves do not break through nor steal" (MATTHEW 6:20). The only things we can take with us through the valley of death are kind deeds, noble thoughts, good character, and forgiven souls. At death, our material possessions will belong to someone else. We shall be stripped of our jewels, and all the temporary things we have known and loved will be left behind.

A wise man will recognize early that it is useless to look for happiness in the passing pleasures of life. If you can't find happiness in your heart, you will never find it in diamonds, clothes, and fancy automobiles. If you fail to find happiness in some humble little house, you would never find it in a magnificent mansion with wall-to-wall carpeting and crystal chandeliers hanging from the ceiling.

Selfishness is a common disease that plagues all humanity. It is the cause of multiplied misery in many human hearts. Selfishness will dwarf the soul and cause life to lose its glow. The burning desire to hold onto what we have, and the constant push to acquire more, has ruined many lives. The smallest package in the whole world is a person all wrapped up in himself.

The biggest obstacle you and I have to overcome is self. John Locke wrote, "The most precious of all possessions is the power over ourselves; power to withstand trial, to bear suffering, to front danger; power over pleasure and pain; power to follow our convictions, however resisted by menace and scorn; the power of calm reliance in scenes of darkness and storms.

He that has not a mastery over his inclinations; he that knows not how to resist the importunity of present pleasure or pain, for the sake of what reason tells him is fit to be done, wants the true principle of virtue and industry, and is in danger of never being good for anything." Life's greatest triumph is victory over self.

Some years ago a very famous man committed suicide. His life, on the surface, appeared to have been very glamorous: he was blessed with many talents and he had made a lot of money; he enjoyed fame and had the admiration of millions of people. In spite of that, he was miserable. He left a letter written for the public which stated, "I have run from country to country, from house to house, and from wife to wife in a ridiculous effort to escape from myself and find happiness. In so doing, I am very much afraid I have brought a great deal of unhappiness to myself and to other people. No one thing is responsible for this suicide, and no one person except myself. I did it because I am fed up with inventing devices for getting through twenty-four hours a day."

What a pity! He had failed to find the meaning and purpose of life. He had tried everything but God, and everything else had failed. He never learned that genuine happiness is gathered from the tree of unselfish service. He didn't even give God a chance.

The familiar phrase, "He lived in his own little world," was used in a story about the death of an old eccentric who had lived in a filth-laden tenement. He had no friends and the neighbors reported that he always stayed by himself. People knew very little about him, but apparently he sometimes ate out of garbage cans and his clothes were ragged.

When the neighbors failed to see the old fellow for several days they called the police. The officers forced their way into his room and found him dead. He had lived and died a recluse. No one knew him and no one loved him; that is, no one except God. In the yellowed newspapers and filthy rags of his room the police found money and stock certificates worth almost seven hundred thousand dollars. That man could have worn the finest of clothes, eaten nourishing food, and lived in the most fashionable section of the city! Instead he chose to live alone.

Little wonder the officers found this message scribbled on a piece of dirty paper: "I am the most miserable man in the world."

So many of us live in houses of fear on foundations of faith that are crumbling away. We move painfully through life with our burdens, forgetful of the power that could be ours. We live in the dirt of spiritual poverty when we could be living in the riches of God's grace.

The only worthy footprints you and I shall leave on the sands of time are what we do for others. What you and I do for ourselves will end when we come to the sunset of life; what we do for others will last forever. If we are to fulfill the purpose of our existence and find happiness in our journey, we must get out of our little world and find the work God wants us to do.

We must travel in the world of human suffering. Have you ever done anything in your life to help ease the pain of a fellow man? We must move out into the world of poverty. Have you made any effort to help feed the multitudes who are starving to death in our chaotic world? We must move out and help the troubled. Perhaps they do not deserve our help, for they may be reaping the fruit of their own ugly sins; but have you tried to help them back to self-respect, or have you found an opportunity to criticize them?

We must move out into the jungle of hate and plant some seeds of love. We need to come out of our ivory towers and help lead the lame and sick souls back to God for spiritual healing. No person can be happy living only unto himself. God made us in such a way that we must share—not only what we are, but what we have as well—with others.

How can we find our way out of our little world of selfishness? How can we learn to move beyond the hot desires that constantly throb in our hearts? What can we do to clear up our blurred vision and see the distant horizons?

First, we must stop blaming our sinful condition on others. No person ever comes to the foot of the cross in search of God's forgiveness as long as he is able to place the responsibility for his chaotic life upon society or upon someone else. You have become the person you are in no small measure because of the choices you have made. No one can force you to be evil any more than someone can force you to live according to God's will. In the final analysis, we make our own decisions. Repentance never grows out of the attitude of "It's really not my fault."

I always have a tender feeling in my heart for those who bear heavy burdens. Some burdens come in the form of handicaps while others are burdens of sorrow or disappointment. And some people are burdened with the guilt that inevitably follows a broken relationship with God.

Once a young lady called and asked if I would give her fifteen minutes of my time. When I asked what she wanted to see me about, she became hysterical. I agreed to see her. She came to my office and told me about an ugly past. At first, she blamed her sins on her family. Then she placed the responsibility upon society. "No one really cared for me," she said. "I just haven't had a chance at life."

She cupped her hands, held her head, and as I watched and listened she sobbed, "What's the use! It's all my fault. The blame is mine. I just want God's forgiveness."

"God can make you clean," I assured her. "Do you believe that God will and can forgive you?" I asked.

"Yes," she replied, and she prayed, "God, forgive me, forgive me!" Needless to say, that repentant girl left with a new heart. Now she is a church-school teacher and a leader in her church.

God stands ready to transform us, but we must be willing to accept His pardon. The road back to spiritual wholeness is an awareness of our need for God. When we go astray, it is our own fault. Paul wrote, ". . . but God is faithful, who will not suffer you to be tempted above that ye are able; but will with the temptation also make a way to escape, that ye may be able to bear it" (I CORINTHIANS 10:13).

Suppose that the prodigal son had refused to return to his father's house? Just suppose that he had said to himself, "It's my brother's fault—he made life miserable for me and I wouldn't be here if he hadn't been so ugly to me"? Suppose that he had blamed his condition on his father? The truth is, the prodigal son knew that no matter what circumstances caused him suddenly to awake and find himself in the far country, the decisions that had brought him to his plight were his own. A realization of that truth was his first step back toward his father's house.

Many people fail to achieve happiness because they refuse to accept themselves for what they are. Most of us are thoroughly proficient in building an oversized ego, and we try to become what we want others to think of us. We look so long and so hard at the ideal self, the self we want to become, that often we feel we have attained the goal. We are afraid to examine ourselves under the lights of reality.

I am constantly telling people, "You can do it. Don't ever give up!" Most of us fail to reach our desired goals because we lack confidence in God and ourselves. On the other hand, there is always the danger that our ambitions will exceed our abilities, and if the goals we set for ourselves are beyond our reach, we may become discontented. We need to recognize our limitations and accept ourselves as we really are. I do not mean that we should settle down in an easy chair of complacency with the attitude of "I can't do it." Most of us could do far more than we are doing if we would use what we have to the best of our ability and stop fretting over what we do not have.

Place the emphasis upon the positive. To become satisfied with what we are and what we have tends to arrest all progress. For example, if you are satisfied with your life as it is, your religious growth will probably stop. Only those who feel discontentment and restlessness ever climb to the spiritual heights of Christian living.

Once we have learned to reconcile ourselves to the inevitable we can do the work God has appointed for us. Fanny Crosby, blind from infancy, refused to hide herself in a world of darkness. No matter what our circumstances may be in life, God has something special for us to do. To look at our handicaps and to dwell on our weak points is to cheat ourselves and fail to do the work God expects us to do. If circumstances beyond our control have brought us to some dark jungle, let us be still and listen for the voice of God. If we are sensitive to Him, I am certain that we will hear Him say to us what He said to Moses: ". . . the place where thou standest is holy ground" (ACTS 7:33).

To move out of our world of selfishness we must learn the art of doing kind deeds for others. We do many gracious things for ourselves and we find little happiness in them. Genuine happiness is ours only when we learn the real meaning of Christian service.

This generation needs to learn the meaning of these profound words of the Master: "For whosoever will save his life shall lose it; but whosoever shall lose his life for my sake and the gospel's, the same shall save it" (MARK 8:35). Jesus was speaking to a people who knew persecution, indictating in unmistakable terms that faithfulness to Christian teachings might cost them their lives. If one renounces the Christian faith in order to save his life, he will surely lose that life in the world to come. On the other hand, if one makes the supreme sacrifice for the Christian life by paying with his own blood, he will find the abundant life in the world to come.

Jesus told the story of a rich man who was so wrapped up in himself that he showed no concern for those who were without food. One year his crops brought forth an abundant harvest, and his barns were entirely too small to store the harvest. In spite of his abundance, he thought only of himself; instead of sharing his goods he built larger barns to save the crop for his future needs. He never knew the joy of sharing his wealth because he could not get out of himself.

The more we are able to get out of ourselves, the more we can serve God. Peter was not always as effective as he could have been in his early days as a disciple because he wanted to project himself into the picture. Judas failed because of his greed, or perhaps because he thought he knew more than Jesus. Our Lord's success was based upon His willingness to listen to God and to trust God completely and fully. Remember that Jesus prayed, "Father, all things are possible unto thee; take away this cup from me: nevertheless not what I will, but what thou wilt" (MARK 14:36).

One Sunday morning a man and his wife walked down the aisle to join the church of which I am the minister. I had visited in the home of the couple and I had the feeling that they were devoted to God and truly Christian. Some days later, I had the opportunity of talking to one of their former pastors. He told me a story about this lovely couple which supported my previous belief.

"When they were members of the church I served," remarked my friend, "the husband taught a Sunday-school class. At that time a little boy in our church was stricken with an incurable disease. It was a long illness, and this man and his wife stood by the lad's family. When the little boy died, the man went to the boy's home and talked with the father. 'I am not a rich man,' he said, 'but I do have some money in the bank, and if you need any of it or all of it to pay expenses or to give this boy a proper burial, it is all yours. You can borrow it or it can be yours permanently.'" That is Christian service; that is religion in action. Such an expression of pure unselfishness is an example of one who has conquered himself and knows how to share his blessings with others.

I suspect that such a man might be surprised when he stands before God and sees a record of his many unselfish deeds. He might wonder when he did so many things for the Master. Jesus will reply, "Inasmuch as ye have done it unto one of the least of these my brethren, ye have done it unto me" (MATTHEW 25:40).

To move out of the stuffy world of selfishness into Christian service and happiness we must do more than recognize that we are responsible for our sins, accept ourselves as we really are, and learn the art of doing kind deeds for others. We must also surrender ourselves to God.

Surrender is entirely up to us. We can move through life bearing the load of unforgiven sins, struggling with our burdens, fighting the baffling problems that will one day defeat us. We can refuse to ask or accept God's help. But God's power is available to every one of us and it is all we need to become the persons God wants us to become. Still, the decision rests with the individual. It is up to you.

Do you remember Ned Langford in *Who Walks Alone?* Ned returned home to a little southern town after serving with the United States Army in the Philippines. He joined his father's business establishment, and he and his lovely fiancée began to plan their future. They had selected a site for their home and then a strange thing happened—Ned noticed some peculiar spots on his shoulder and arm. The local physician suggested that he see another doctor, so Ned went to St. Louis and consulted an Army surgeon. The doctor knew immediately that Ned had leprosy, and he knew the agony and despair that would fill the young man's heart when he gave him the diagnosis. After a few minutes, the doctor looked Ned in the face and said, "You have to do this, soldier, whether you are scared or not. You can take it standing up and fighting, or you can lie down and let it beat you—and you're the only one who can say about that." Then he proceeded to describe the restrictions and the treatment of the dreaded disease.

Ned knew his dreams were shattered: he could never go home again. Many times he wanted to give up in despair but each time he could hear the words of the doctor: "You can take it standing up and fighting, or you can lie down and let it beat you—and you're the only one who can say about that."

Ned went back to the Philippines and entered a leper colony. He began his life of sacrificial service. He encouraged other lepers, and helped to establish a power plant in the colony, and was a key person in instituting some fisheries. He lived in the colony for twenty-five years, always serving others.

Some of the others were being cured, but Ned was slowly dying. Finally the day came when he was to sail back to America. He was going to a leprosarium in Louisiana to live the last days of his life. His train passed through his hometown one night and Ned lifted the shade and looked out, and in the moonlight he saw the place he had loved. In his soul flags of triumph were waving. He had been a man—he had not failed. He heard again the words of the old doctor: ". . . you're the only one who can say about that."

The Master is saying to each of us, "You need not fail. The cross is your assurance of victory. Your sins can be forgiven. Your evil habits can be broken. Your ways can be transformed." He spoke to all of us when He said to the woman, "Thy sins are forgiven. Go and sin no more." We are not hopelessly bound by selfishness. We can be free again to live fruitfully, love fully, and serve gladly. When you and I place ourselves completely at God's disposal, He will surely make it come to pass. Why not try it!

8

When Life
Blows Up in Your Face

"WHAT DO YOU do when life blows up in your face?" an attractive young woman asked. That is a good question. It has been asked by thousands of frustrated people. "Go to God," I advised, "and get your orders from Him." There are always two roads open to us when we face a crisis—ours and God's.

During the week before Jesus faced the cross He was hailed by the shouting multitude as their King. This was a procession, and it looked like the beginning of a new day. Christ was the real Hero in Jerusalem on that first Palm Sunday. Even the Pharisees and scribes seemed near the point of admitting defeat. Hatred filled their hearts and they wanted Him out of the way, but "they feared the multitude" (MATTHEW 21:46).

Only a few short days after His triumphant entry into Jerusalem the shadow of the cross fell in Jesus' path. Suddenly the shouts of "Hosanna to the son of David: Blessed is he that cometh in the name of the Lord" (MATTHEW 21:9) changed to "Crucify Him! Crucify Him!" It looked as though His world were blowing up in His face. Christ had lived a perfect life. He had healed the sick, restored sight to the blind, loved the unlovable, and forgiven the ugly sins of many. In spite of that, He faced a cruel cross. What did Jesus do?

1. Most important of all, He did not abandon His faith in God. He refused to give up in defeat at the first sign of suffering and opposition.

I know a man who, until recently, lived a respectable life. He had no real convictions about God, and therefore had never surrendered his life to Him. Suddenly, he faced a crisis and because he had not developed a firm faith in God he became utterly frustrated. He prayed, demanding certain things from God, but when God refused to meet his demands the man became bitter and his weak faith shattered. Then after months of sincere prayer, he gave himself completely to God and found the strength to accept life with confidence. When the cross was evident, Jesus did not forsake His faith; rather, it helped him face life unafraid.

2. Jesus prayed about His situation. He did not have a martyr-complex; He had a keen sense of the worth of life. At first, Jesus prayed that He could evade the cross—this was a natural prayer because no normal person delights in sheer agony and pain. When it was evident that the cross could not be bypassed, Jesus prayed for the strength He would need in order to be faithful: ". . . nevertheless not what I will, but what thou wilt" (MARK 14:36). Jesus knew that it was far more important to do God's will than to be free from pain. He was determined to be faithful at any cost.

3. Finally, Jesus expressed His complete trust in God. Our Lord was not afraid; He was certain that any obstacle in the path of life which could not be removed could be endured and conquered. He had expressed this faith to His disciples: ". . . be of good cheer; I have overcome the world" (JOHN 16:33). Not only do we have the promise that we can overcome the world, but we believe God can cause the obstacles of life to become stepping-stones to spiritual growth.

Once Jesus and His disciples were crossing the Sea of Galilee and the Master, weary from a long day, had fallen asleep. As they rowed away from the shore the sea was calm and the reflection of the high mountains played in the water. The Sea of Galilee is surrounded by mountains and it is almost seven hundred feet below sea level. But as the wind whips over the mountains the placid-looking waters can suddenly become mountains of turbulent waves that frighten even an experienced seaman.

The unpredictable nature of this body of water is a parable of what often happens in life. One moment the stars are bright and the breezes gentle, and the next moment we find ourselves sailing under cloudy skies in the midst of a sudden and violent storm. How quickly the storms of sickness, disappointment, and even death gather on the horizon! Some of the storms of life make us afraid. We become aware of the fact that we are not strong enough to face or endure them. We see clearly our inadequacy to face them without God.

When the disciples heard the waves splashing against the little boat and felt the water spill over onto them, they spoke out of fright, "Lord, save us: we perish" (MATTHEW 8:25). Jesus was asleep but when He awoke He was Master of the storm. He gave the disciples peace within and without, and they marveled because the winds and sea obeyed His words.

There are times in life when God does not choose to still the storm, but He never leaves us alone. He will always break through our fears if we will permit Him to speak to us. He will instill within us the confidence that comes from an awareness of the power and presence of God. The storms may continue to rage but we become acutely aware of the fact that His grace is sufficient for us.

Humanity must learn to accept the inevitable and build a philosophy that includes the inescapable experiences of life. In all of life we need not fear as long as we are committed to God. He has assured us of victory, and the light of His love will shine in every dark valley. His strength can be ours when the load is heavy. When we are struggling under the weight of ugly sins, God's forgiveness can be ours. When we learn to trust God and accept the inevitable, we can say with the Psalmist, "Yea, though I walk through the valley of the shadow of death, I will fear no evil: for thou art with me; thy rod and thy staff they comfort me" (23:4).

Not only must we learn to accept the inevitable experiences of life, but we must also become aware of God's power to make us triumphant. When the Psalmist was meditating on the greatness and goodness of God he was compelled to say, "Such knowledge is too wonderful for me; it is high, I cannot attain unto it" (139:6).

Trials and tribulations in life are inevitable; we must expect them. But through Christ you and I can overcome the trials of this world; and with Christ we can be triumphant.

Life often weaves a confusing web. In spite of our theology

and philosophy, much of what happens to us is shrouded in mystery. Logic cannot explain it, reason is often a stumbling block. The only penetrating force into some of the hard experiences of life is an unwavering faith in a sovereign God, a faith that proclaims His goodness, love, mercy, and power.

When Jesus hung on the cross He said, "My God, my God, why hast thou forsaken me?" (MARK 15:34). Some feel that Jesus was quoting Scripture (PSALM 22:1). This may be true, but I believe that Jesus felt—at least for the moment—forsaken. Our Lord knew all the dark valleys through which humanity must walk. He endured even more of life's sorrows, sufferings, disappointments, and trouble than we shall ever know, yet He was triumphant. We need not feel defeated, because the same source of power that was available to Jesus can be ours. The truth is, we may not understand some of the burdens that fall upon us, but we can endure them and have peace of mind while carrying them. This is God's promise.

Man's only sustaining hope—a hope that will neither fail nor fade—is his hope in God. The Psalmist wrote, "Happy is he . . . whose hope is in the Lord his God" (146:5). I have seen strong men and women place their hope in wealth, and before the journey ends discover that wealth is not sufficient to satisfy the deep longings of the soul. I have seen others place their hope in knowledge, only to be disappointed when knowledge fails to bring peace of mind. I have seen others anchor their hope in position, but in a time of crisis position leaves one empty and void. Better than knowledge, wealth, and all the thrills of life is an unswerving faith in God. The writer of Proverbs penned a gem when he wrote, "Better is a little with righteousness than great revenues without right" (16:8).

No wonder so many people are afraid of life. To battle the storms of life with our hope resting only in the trivial and temporary will bring us to despair and defeat. God didn't make us to live in the gutter of spiritual poverty; He made us to climb the rugged slopes of unselfishness and to live on plateaus of love, understanding, and forgiveness where the air is fresh and the sun bright. We won't know any peace or happiness until we at least begin to climb.

When I was only a lad, my brothers and I tried to start a

high-powered gasoline engine with kerosene. It sputtered, popped, and smoked, but it wouldn't run with any degree of efficiency. We discovered that we just couldn't operate a gasoline engine on kerosene. The reason is obvious—the engine was not made to burn kerosene. Life is like that. You can't live a happy, satisfying life by just making money, running from one cocktail party to another, and working constantly to stay on the top rung of the social ladder. The reason ought to be obvious: God didn't make us for such a life. If we are to become the persons God created, we must give ourselves to God and place our hope in Him. When our dreams are falling apart and our cross is heavy, we must continue to hope. We shall never gain any strength for the journey by abandoning our faith.

A man called me recently for an appointment. He was well-educated, had a fine position, and was admired by many of his fellow employees. In spite of this, he found life dull and drab. "There is nothing left," he said, "to make me want to keep going. The future looks empty and desolate."

There was no question about this man's life; he had some heavy burdens and his problems were perplexing. "Since you do not understand life," I replied, "you have decided that life is not worth the struggle! God gave you life and He can make it worthwhile. His power, working in and through your life, can place a star of hope in the darkest night. God does not always deliver us from the storm, but He gives us power to keep going."

Many years ago Maxwell N. Cornelius wrote some lines that ought to give us hope when our vision is blurred:

> Not now, but in the coming years,
>   It may be in the better land,
> We'll read the meaning of our tears,
>   And there, sometime, we'll understand.
>
> Then trust in God thro' all the days;
>   Fear not, for He doth hold thy hand;
> Though dark the way, still sing and praise,
>   Sometime, sometime, we'll understand.

Why what we long for most of all,
Eludes so oft our eager hand;
Why hopes are crushed and castles fall,
Up there, sometime, we'll understand.

Don't become discouraged when the load is heavy, because God's strength is adequate and His hand will steady you. To admit life is no longer worth living is another way of saying, "My strength is not sufficient for the journey." Why not take the next step and admit to yourself that God is able to supply all you need in order to face life without fear?

Often we become impatient when life does not go according to our plans. We forget that God is sovereign and His purposes and plans will be achieved. In *Healing Words*, Dr. Charles L. Allen has reminded us that God " . . . has an entire eternity to work His plans. So don't become bitter—if time does not set you to singing, eternity will."

In Psalm 38 the Psalmist reveals unto us the agony of his heart. He freely admits his sins and tells God that he is sorry. His burdens are heavy and his troubles are great. His relatives and friends have deserted him and the light in his eye has faded. He wants forgiveness. Forgetting his pride, he cries, ". . . my strength faileth me . . ." (v. 10).

Forsaken by everyone else, the Psalmist then turns to God. Here he anchors his hope: "For in thee, O Lord, do I hope: thou wilt hear, O Lord my God" (v. 15). He prays in perfect confidence. He didn't say, "O Lord, I hope You will hear me"; he prayed, " . . . thou wilt hear." There are times in every life when there is only one place to go for the help we need. When others fail us we can find help in God.

"What next?" asked a high-school senior. "Should I go to college, or should I take the first job I can find?" His words represented more fear than cynicism. Many of our young men and women graduating from high school today have lived each day listening to news analysts and scientists paint a rather dim picture of the future. Tensions of the last three decades have been appalling. We hear of "mega-death" and "total oblitera-tion." We talk of peace, and yet the strong nations of the world prepare for war. Little wonder there is an attitude of "What's the use?" on the part of some of our youth.

If we want to face life with confidence we must remember that God made us for eternity. If, through the foolishness of man, the human race is to be annihilated, let us live now in such a way that every stroke counts for good. Should our time be short or long, let us approach God's throne with evidence that the tools of love, concern, and forgiveness have been used. Each day brings a task from God, and it is our responsibility to give life our best.

If we want to face life with confidence we must be armed with some convictions about our existence. Only faith in God can break the bars of fear and make us free.

1. God is behind life; that is to say, you and I are not here by mere chance. We live because God willed for us to live. Human life is the direct result of a divine order. The Psalmist said, "Thou hast beset me behind and before . . ." (139:5). We do not use this little word *beset* very much, but it is a powerful word. It means that God has surrounded us; we are hemmed in by His love and mercy. I find comfort in that thought.

No one could ever convince me that this marvelous thing called personality is an accident. God planned our existence and only as we find our purpose in Him shall we discover the thrill of the journey.

As long as we know that God stands behind us, the struggle is not in vain. Our faith teaches us that we are moving toward a heavenly port. The seas may be rough at times but God does not send us out on a hopeless voyage. Somewhere in the distance we shall find the warm lights of the harbor where we can rest from the sorrows, fears, and burdens of the trip.

When William Cowper found himself in deep despair, he spent more than an hour riding through the streets of London in search of the river, where he intended to end his earthly journey. The fog that night was so thick that the horse-drawn cab moved slowly and the river was nowhere in sight. In desperation Cowper rebuked the driver and thrust open the door of the cab—only to find himself back at his own doorstep! He went quickly to his room, took his quill in hand, and penned his famous poem "Light Shining Out of Darkness." There is a particular message for us in some of the lines:

> God moves in a mysterious way
> His wonders to perform;
> He plants his footsteps in the sea,
> And rides upon the storm.
>
> Judge not the Lord by feeble sense,
> But trust him for his grace;
> Behind a frowning providence
> He hides a shining face.

2. Our fears subside when we face each day armed with the belief that God is in life. The one thing of which I am certain is that God has not left us as strangers in a hopeless world. The Psalmist felt his heart uplifted when he became aware of the fact that God had His "hand upon me."

I frequently talk with people who have the feeling that they are castaways on the sea of life. Some months ago I read about a ship drifting helplessly in the Atlantic Ocean. An uncontrollable fire had caused the crew to abandon the ship and it drifted for several days in rough seas at the mercy of the winds and currents. We are not at the mercy of the circumstances of life. We claim a God who loves us and cares for us, a God from whom we cannot hide or escape.

I spend a great deal of my time going in and out of hospitals. I see a lot of suffering and sorrow. There are times when faith is weak and people find it easy to blame God for sickness. I am constantly telling people that God is not the cause of our suffering, but that He is in it with us.

When Jesus died on the cross He was not alone. God was there and His heart was bleeding too. Let us never forget that God is always within reach. "For we have not an high priest which cannot be touched with the feeling of our infirmities . . ." (HEBREWS 4:15).

Recently, I was thrilled by the faith of a young couple. I walked into a hospital room where a little three-year-old boy clasped his arms around his father's neck. The mother, weary from the many long nights she had stayed by her child's bed-side, sat in an overstuffed chair in the corner. For the moment, the lad felt pretty well. Some months before, a physician had discovered cancer in one of his kidneys; this kidney was removed. Then cancer was found in the other kidney and in both lungs. This little boy doesn't have much time left on earth unless God intervenes.

The parents and I talked about life and the hope that the Christian faith proclaims. "There are a lot of things we do not understand about life," I remarked. "There are times when the heart throbs with joy and we know life is good; and then there are days when the storms come. Yet, we know God is in life and He will never forsake us."

"We do not understand this," the mother replied. Looking toward her husband and little boy, she said, "But we are sure that God's hand is in this." Her husband nodded his assent to her courageous words. "We have sensed His presence and we believe, though we do not understand, the words of Paul, ' . . . that all things work together for good to them that love God.' "

As long as we face life armed with the sure knowledge that God is in it, we need not be afraid. We are likely to experience tribulation, distress, persecution, and peril. Surely we will know loneliness, hurt, and even death. None of these will be able to separate us from God. Paul wrote in such a convincing way that ". . . in all these things we are more than conquerors through him that loved us" (ROMANS 8:37).

3. I always tell people that through God we can master life. The trouble with most people is that they try to manage their lives without giving God a chance to help them. When we come to the end of all the human strength we can muster, God is standing there waiting to help us.

There is a kind of faith and courage that will never permit a person to go down in utter defeat. That is the kind of courage Jesus knew when He faced the cross. Such courage will enable us to be victorious, too, when we feel the burden on our shoulders.

You cannot evade temptation, but with God's help you can overcome it. Perhaps it is impossible for us to keep evil thoughts from erupting into the conscious mind, but through

God's grace we can keep them from living there. We need not be afraid of life as long as we hold the Father's hand.

As a boy I made many trips to a little country store about two hundred yards from our home. It was a pleasant journey during the day, but after the sun hid its face I dreaded the trip. Many times my mother or father would walk to the mailbox with me and wait there until I returned. I would take a flashlight and hurry to the store, and all the while I was within sight of home. It was a real comfort to know that my mother or father could see me every step of the way. I could not see them, but they could see me. So God is always upon the human scene. He watches us and knows every step we take as well as every thought hidden deep within our minds.

I remember talking to a woman who was gripped with fear. "I can't find any reason for living," she said. I suppose that in every life there are times when the purpose is blurred. This woman had been deeply hurt, and after talking with her for a while, I discovered that she had based her faith in God upon her faith in man; that is to say, her faith in God was limited by her faith in man. She had been disappointed by one in whom she had placed her confidence, and since a loved one had betrayed her, she also felt that God had deserted her.

Man must never be our guide for our faith in God. Man is subject to selfish desires and he often changes. But our faith in man ought to be based on our faith in God, for the God we see reflected in Christ is the only reliable force in our world. "Jesus Christ the same yesterday, and to day, and for ever" (HEBREWS 13:8).

Jesus died on the cross, deceived by one of His own disciples. He died a victim of dirty hands and evil hearts. In spite of the fact that our Lord was betrayed by men, Jesus held onto His faith in God. Man tricked Him but God stood by Him.

4. There are many mysteries in each tomorrow, but there is one thing of which we can be certain: God stands in each tomorrow. The only way to have our tomorrows free from fear is to walk with God today. When the grime of sorrow blights our dreams and the gritty whirlwinds of disappointment fill our hearts with fear, we must fortify ourselves with our faith that God stands in each tomorrow. John Greenleaf Whittier expressed this unswerving faith in God's goodness:

> I know not what the future hath
> Of marvel or surprise,
> Assured alone that life and death
> God's mercy underlies.

Once we commit ourselves to God, we need not fear the future. It is true, we cannot see the future; we do not know what will be ours tomorrow. But this arrangement grows out of God's wisdom. If we knew the joys of the future we would miss the beauty of this day. On the other hand, if we knew the sorrows of tomorrow we would not find any gladness in today.

A well-known story describes two British businessmen who were discussing the greatest desire of their hearts. One asked his companion, "If you could have anything in the world you wanted, what would it be?" The other replied, after a few minutes of serious consideration, "I would ask for a copy of the *London Times*, dated ten years from now." The man's request was granted. Given the *London Times* dated one decade in advance, he nervously thumbed through it and found the quotations of the stock market. He saw an opportunity to make millions of pounds. Throwing the paper down, he started to rush out to purchase certain stocks, but as the paper fell to the floor he noticed that the back page contained the obituary column. He was shocked to discover his own name at the top of the list. God, in His infinite wisdom, knew that it would not be good to permit us to see the future.

It should be sufficient to know that God stands ready to guide us safely through each experience. Jesus was never afraid of life. He knew that God was good and wise—and that was all He needed to know.

I remember a woman who, for several years, had walked down a dark and lonely path. She endured more sorrow and sickness than any other person I have ever known. In spite of all her trouble she kept her faith in God. Some people wondered, "How does she keep going?" Each day she prayed, asking God to give her strength for the day, and God never failed her. One day she said, "The Christian life is the only way to live. I know this is true and I will never retreat. Somewhere down the road I know I shall feel the touch of the Master's hand."

What a challenge! Let us do what we know is right, regardless of the circumstances of life. The road may be hard, but somewhere along the path I am confident that you and I shall feel the gentle touch of the Master's hand, and then we shall know that all is well and we have not lived in vain. Face life! Live fully! Trust God completely and He will guide you safely through. Don't be afraid.

9

Five Ways
to Grow Spiritually

EVERYBODY WOULD LIKE to have spiritual serenity but few are willing to work diligently to achieve it. The glitter of materialism casts a shadow over the eternal values and we become content with respectability—which in our generation is far short of any worthwhile divine achievement. We become satisfied with wading in the muddy water of what society has stamped "acceptable," and have little desire to swim in the pure water that flows from the throne of God.

Growing spiritually can be compared with planting and cultivating a flower garden. First, the ground must be prepared; then the seeds and plants must be placed carefully in the ground; constant care must follow. The garden will require warm days, sunshine, water, and cultivation. The weeds must be pulled out almost daily or the garden will lose its beauty.

For several years my wife and I visited a gracious lady who always grew beautiful flowers. Her yard was ablaze with glowing color. Now she has moved on to the Father's house and I suspect she has a beautiful garden there. Last spring we passed the house where our friend had lived and we saw only a straggling flower in bloom here and there in the yard. The weeds had just about taken over.

Unless we give regular attention to the garden of the soul, it will not be long before life will turn into a savage jungle. Instead of kind thoughts, Christian deeds, and compassion for others, we will discover the weeds of selfishness, the briers of greed, and the ugly bushes of evil.

The fact that a beautiful garden is a matter of constant care was brought home to me in a very forceful way while I was visiting an old friend who grows a profusion of lovely flowers. One day, just as the sun was setting, I asked, "What is your secret for growing these beautiful flowers?" Without hesitation she replied, "Some say it's because I have a green thumb, but this is not true. I tell folks they can grow flowers like these if they are willing to work among them. The only secret I have is hard work."

What is the secret of spiritual growth? If we are to become radiant individuals there are certain rules we must obey. First, we must have a dominant desire to be a radiant person. We shall never achieve greatness in spirit unless we desire it, and no person has ever attained spiritual maturity by accident. Dr. William Sangster wrote, "All people come to God unclean." Spiritual growth begins with a desire to be a better person. This causes us to repent of our sins and to accept Jesus as our Saviour.

Unfortunately some people feel joining a church is about all they must do to become radiant. One might as well say that visits to a doctor's waiting room will keep people strong and healthy. Joining the church may not add one iota to one's spiritual growth. I have known people who joined the church and never attend, yet all the time think they are in good standing with the Lord. I am certain that God will not look at the church membership rolls when we stand before Him to be judged.

Then comes the period of constant care and cultivation. If we are to grow spiritually, there are at least five things we must do: (1) spend some time in prayer each day; (2) worship God and read the Bible regularly; (3) love God and others with all our beings; (4) serve gladly; (5) be completely obedient to the will of God.

1. No one advances in the school of spiritual growth without fervent prayer. One must find some time each day to commune with God. Most church people have a confused idea of prayer.

Effective prayer takes place when man's spirit and God's Spirit come together. Prayer is not a monologue; it is conversation with God.

Conversation requires two persons; each does some of the talking and some of the listening. How many of us wait upon God to speak to us after we have finished praying? Most of our prayers are shallow; we pray for the things we want and have little concern for the hurts of the world.

Some of us have dug shallow wells of prayer and we do not find prayer very satisfying. Paul advised, "Pray without ceasing" (I THESSALONIANS 5:17). Certainly he did not mean for us to give up everything else and spend all our time in prayer—he was a hard-working and practical man. I think Paul meant for us to live in *a spirit of prayer*. When we live in an atmosphere of prayer it will be difficult to take advantage of our fellow man or to mistreat the stranger whose path crosses ours.

I encourage people to develop prayer habits. For example, select something that you do each day which requires your physical strength but not your power of concentration, and use the moments spent at this task for prayer. A housewife might try praying while she makes the beds or washes the dishes. A man might use the time for prayer while he is shaving or dressing or driving to work.

I spend a lot of time in an automobile. I always pray when I stop at a traffic light, and it keeps me from becoming impatient; it also keeps me in the right frame of mind. I have developed the habit of praying while riding in elevators. I direct a simple prayer for myself and for someone who may be in the elevator with me.

I think most of us would be astonished to discover how many minutes we waste each day, but the wise person will use these minutes. I do not believe that this type of praying is sufficient, but it will build a strong spiritual fiber within your soul.

Dr. William Sangster spent much of his time in prayer. He said, ". . . let these unpremeditated prayers all be extras, not substitutes. Growth in the mind of Christ demands iron firmness with ourselves in our fixed periods of prayer."

Jesus said, ". . . when thou prayest, enter into thy closet, and when thou hast shut thy door, pray to thy Father which is in secret . . ." (MATTHEW 6:6). We can concentrate better when we shut out the noise of the world. We know how to pray better when we are alone with the Father.

If we are really serious about achieving a new level of spiritual growth, we must pray. We must give God some of the first minutes of the early morning; let us ask Him to guide us through the day. Each day is different and will present new opportunities. If we pray, God can guard us from selfishness and keep us from facing the sunset with a heart full of regrets.

Let our last waking minutes also be spent in the presence of God. I never close my eyes to sleep without talking to God, asking for His forgiveness for any deed, thought, or attitude that may not have been in harmony with His will.

2. Spiritual growth takes place as a result of worship and of reading the Bible. "You can worship anywhere" is a phrase I often hear. The person who likes to play golf insists that he can worship as fervently on the golf course as in the sanctuary. The family who enjoy the lake will tell you that they can feel God's presence in a boat as much as in church. I am well aware of the fact that God is not confined to the sanctuary. I know one can feel His presence in the beauty of nature, in the crowded street, or in the quiet of a lovely church; but the fact is, I worship God best in His church, and I believe most people have had the same experience.

The person who is serious about the Christian life will find his way to God's house as often as possible. I would suggest that the best place to make decisions that will, in some measure, determine one's destiny is in the quiet of a church. Jesus, according to the Scripture, was a regular Visitor to the house of God. Our Father has given each of us seven days a week and He has commanded us to keep one of them holy.

The person who has committed himself to Christ will feel that it is not only his duty but his privilege to worship each week. I recently visited a family stricken by sickness. The wife had just come home from the hospital and her husband remarked, "We shall miss church this Sunday." They have missed only about two Sundays since joining the church which I now serve. The wife said, "As soon as I am able to go anywhere, I will be back in church. We don't let anything interfere with going to church." These people truly are growing Christians. It would be hard to convince me that a person who places church attendance after relaxation and recreation is really concerned about Christian growth.

We grow spiritually by regularly reading the Bible. This book is still the best seller, but I wonder how many people read it any more. We believe that the Bible is the Word of God, and in it we can find complete instructions as to how we ought to live as Christians. It teaches us how to treat each other and gives us a clear picture of the way Jesus lived. It should be the aim of every Christian to face life with the same poise, convictions, and peace that were evident in the life of Jesus.

During World War I Henry Ford and Woodrow Wilson made a pledge to read a chapter in the Bible each day. Commenting on this after the death of President Wilson, Ford said, "I have kept my pledge and I understand that Wilson kept it, too."

John Quincy Adams wrote in his diary on September 26, 1816, "I have made it a practice for several years to read the Bible through in the course of every year. I usually devote to this reading the first hour after I rise every morning."

The Bible is truly the Christian's textbook. It is a reliable guide that will inspire and guide us through life, but it becomes effective only when we apply it to our thoughts, words, and deeds. An Indian Brahman once said to a missionary, "If you Christians in India were like your Book, you would conquer India in five years."

3. It is impossible for spiritual growth to take place except in the soil of love. Love is the basis for all good. Jesus once said, in response to a lawyer's question concerning what one must do to inherit eternal life, ". . . love the Lord thy God with all thy heart, and with all thy soul, and with all thy strength, and with all thy mind; and thy neighbor as thyself" (LUKE 10:27). It is impossible to be a Christian unless love reigns supreme in the human heart.

Jesus placed love of God first. It will be impossible for us to love others as we should until we love God with all our beings.

Once we have made contact with the love of God, and when this divine love flows through our lives, we can love our enemies and our neighbors as we love ourselves.

Some people live under the misapprehension that love is merely the absence of hate, resentment, and jealousy. This is not true. Of course, there can be no love when these monsters are present, but genuine love is far more than the absence of our prejudices. There are a host of people against whom we hold no resentment; we are not jealous of them, either, but love itself is absent. You see, love must be positive.

There are no conditions that dictate to love. It is supreme. For example, Jesus did not say, "Love God in fair weather." He intended for us to love God during the storms of life, too. Jesus did not say, "Love your neighbor when he is a good neighbor." Jesus commanded us to love others even when they do not deserve love. Jesus did not say, "Love God as long as you get your way and as long as you understand life." Jesus wanted us to love God even when all our prayers are answered in the negative, and to trust God even when life seems to be the victim of evil forces.

Do you suppose the disciples could make sense out of the cross? There was the best Man who ever lived—falsely accused and savagely beaten and nailed to a cross! He had never wronged any man and the record of His life could have been described by one word: *love*. Yet He suffered. He died. It just didn't make sense. Do you suppose the disciples asked themselves, "Why? Why did this happen to our Lord?"

Standing at the foot of the cross one can see the results of evil. Here goodness and love are crucified by all the evil and hate in the world. Justice seems forsaken and evil appears to reign. Yet, even in this, God had a plan. When we stand three days away from Calvary we can see God's divine plan at work: He proved to the world that love and goodness will triumph.

Do you believe that love will triumph? I have never seen hate and evil win. Jesus commanded us to love—that's all, but that's enough! When we love God with our total being, and our neighbors as ourselves, God will take care of the rest.

4. We grow spiritually when we serve. There are no idle Christians; the person who is committed to Christ is busy work-

ing to promote God's Kingdom. The person who wants to grow more mature in the Christian life will not wait until someone asks him to do something; he will find something that needs to be done.

There are dangers in simply working in the church. Some folks work in the church for the wrong reasons, enjoying the credit and praise they receive from others. They do not work for the glory of God but for the satisfaction they derive from their efforts. We must keep in mind that we are not necessarily Christians because we work in the church. The truth is, we work in the church *because we are Christians.*

Jesus had something to say about this. He warned against praying as the hypocrites did—they loved to stand in the synagogues and on the street corners in order that others might notice them. Jesus said, ". . . They have their reward" (MATTHEW 6:5); that is to say, the praise men gave them was their reward. God does not honor such prayers.

Jesus said, "Wherefore by their fruits ye shall know them" (MATTHEW 7:20). Therefore, one mark of the growing Christian is service. Jesus also said, "Let your light so shine before men, that they may see your good works, and glorify your Father which is in heaven" (MATTHEW 5:16). We serve, if we are genuinely devoted to Christ, not for our own sake but to glorify God.

Everyone can do something. We may not all be able to teach a Sunday-school class, or sing in the choir, or participate in group discussions, but this does not mean that we are of no value to God through the church. We can pray. We can be present. We can invite our neighbors to church. We can, with God's help, be the persons He wants us to be.

One of my favorite stories is recorded in Acts. Only a passing reference is made to a woman named Dorcas and her life did not make the headlines. She was not, by some standards, an outstanding churchwoman and probably never stood in public to pray or speak before an audience.

One day Dorcas became ill and died. Her friends sent for Peter to come and help them. When Peter arrived, most of the people of Joppa were crowded into the humble house in which Dorcas had lived. They were weeping and many of them brought coats and garments that Dorcas had made for them. What a noble tribute! There were many things that Dorcas could not do, but she did whatever she could. We sometimes forget that all service ranks the same in the eyes of God.

Genuine service is rendered only for the sake of fulfilling a need. The person who serves from honest motives doesn't care who gets the credit as long as the need is met.

5. A growing Christian must be obedient to God. There is always a struggle when human nature longs for something that is in conflict with God's will. One major trouble with the world today is the fact that we work for what we want instead of what we need.

Obedience must rest on the foundation of faith. Before we can be obedient to God we must come to trust Him as a loving, all-wise, heavenly Father. It is impossible to trust someone in whom we have little confidence. We must be willing to follow the commands of God even though we do not understand them.

I made the statement once that Jesus may not have understood why it was necessary for Him to go to the cross. I received many letters from people who took exception to this view. My reasoning was that, if Jesus fully understood, He would not have prayed for some other way. Jesus prayed, ". . . if thou be willing, remove this cup from me . . ." (LUKE 22:42). Such a view does not minimize the stature of our Lord; it magnifies His complete faith in the goodness and wisdom of God. Jesus continued, ". . . nevertheless not my will, but thine, be done." Jesus was saying, "Father, I yield to Your wishes. I do not relish the idea of suffering on the cross, but if this is what it takes to complete Your plan for My life, I am willing to do it."

The person who wants to be mature in the Christian life must grow to the point where his will and God's will are one and the same. This means a complete abandonment of self. Our desires and wishes are subdued by God's plan for us. In the final analysis, we must want what is best for us, and only God knows what is best.

Life is a journey and if we are to march unafraid we must place our trust in God. When things go wrong we are likely to demand an explanation from Him. We want to know why. We may find, after much struggle, a satisfactory answer to some of life's tragedies, but there are many experiences we may face for which there are no reasonable answers. At those times we must believe that "all things work together for good to them that love God" (ROMANS 8:28).

Genuine obedience, like love, does not seek to explain life in logical terms; we are obedient when all our energy is concentrated on doing what we think God wants us to do. We do not obey God because we feel that to do so will give us a place of advantage in the sight of God. Rather, we obey God because we believe that He is good and wise.

When this great country of ours was in its infancy, the following advertisement is reputed to have appeared in France to persuade French priests to volunteer for service in the new world: "We offer you no salary, no recompense, no holidays, no pension; but much hard work, a poor dwelling, few consolations, many disappointments, frequent sickness, a violent and lonely death, an unknown grave."

We obey God, not for what He does for us, but because we believe that obedience is the only way to reach our destiny.

10

From Despair to Triumph

I HAVE SEEN numerous people who are living in rooms of gloom and defeat. Most of them will spend the rest of their existence in despair unless they try to make their lives count for something good and noble.

Many people need to learn that defeat is an attitude, not necessarily a condition. Most of us have failed to live up to God's expectations. We stumble and falter along the trail, but as long as we find the courage and inspiration to get up and try again, we are not defeated. One historian, writing about the Civil War, made this comment: "Lee's army was defeated at Gettysburg, but not Lee." The least desirable street in the world upon which we can pitch our tents is the street named "Defeat." Henry Wadsworth Longfellow wrote:

> Not in the clamor of the crowded street,
> Not in the shouts and plaudits of the throng,
> But in ourselves, are triumph and defeat.

Pastor Martin Niemöller and his "stubborn faith," as the Nazis called it, will be remembered as long as men talk about saints. He, along with a few other Christians, spoke out against Hitler and his godless regime. Niemoeller was arrested and thrown into prison, where he was given a chance to sign a letter indicating that he had made a mistake in opposing Hitler. It would have assured his release, but Pastor Niemoeller emphatically refused. Leo Stein, who was in prison with Niemoeller, tells us that this faithful disciple remarked to a Gestapo official, "I will have to disappoint you. . . . As I have already stated, again and again, I desire only to keep my conscience clear before my God."

Men died by the thousands in German concentration camps. They were beaten and tortured and suffered agonies beyond description. At one point, when hope appeared defeated, one man looked at Niemöller and asked, "What shall we do, what shall we do?" Niemöller stood for a moment in silence and then he said, "Brothers in Christ, don't despair. We must not weaken, even for a second. God will give us strength to show His power to His enemies. We may lose our lives, but we will save our souls." Even in defeat, God will supply the courage and strength men need to stand as faithful soldiers.

At one time, defeat was so evident among the prisoners that one man shouted, "What is going to become of us? Has God forgotten us?" Again it was Martin Niemöller who spoke: "God hasn't forgotten you. God never forgets. Remember it is more important to die as Christians than to live in cowardice."

Here is something we can all cling to when defeat seems near. Niemöller was willing to admit that the future looked dim, that death might come the next hour, but even death would not defeat him. He would be victorious over death because he was faithful to God. The Christian church would assume its rightful place in our century if there were more people whose daily litany was, "I would prefer to die on duty than to live as a coward."

History is filled with glittering stories of people who marched from failure to victory because they refused to accept defeat as a permanent condition of their lives. Many times I think of the words of Isaac Watts:

> Our God, our help in ages past,
>   Our hope in years to come,
> Be thou our guard while troubles last,
>   And our eternal home.
>
> Under the shadow of thy throne
>   Thy saints have dwelt secure;
> Sufficient is thine arm alone,
>   And our defense is sure.

Mozart looked at life through the window of poverty. No one would have criticized him had he taken the attitude that he was defeated and could not possibly make a contribution to civilization. But in spite of the fact that he was destined to be buried in a pauper's grave, and although his days on earth were plagued by monetary hardship, Mozart worked determinedly to set down on paper the notes of the beautiful music he left to the world—music we often use in our church services to glorify God.

Oliver Goldsmith applied for a job at a naval hospital and was flatly rejected. He did not accept this as utter defeat; he went away and wrote *The Vicar of Wakefield*. Despite his struggles, Goldsmith was able to write, "In all my griefs—and God has given me my share—I still had hopes. . . ." As long as we can hang onto our hopes, God will provide a way out of defeat.

One day, in the midst of writing a book, Dr. A. J. Cronin convinced himself that he was a failure. He told himself that his efforts were wasted, that even the thought that he could write anything worth reading was sheer futility. He took his manuscript and cast it into a trash barrel. Later, while walking, he came upon Angus, an old farmer who approved of Cronin's work as an author. Angus was digging in a bog, trying to rescue it from the swamp. When Cronin told him that he had given up the idea of writing, Angus looked at him in disappointment and contempt. For a moment he was silent, and then he said, "No doubt you're the one that's right, Doctor, and I'm the one that's wrong. My father ditched this bog all his days and never made a pasture. I've dug it all my days and I've never made a pasture. But pasture or no pasture, I cannot help but dig; for my father knew and I know that if you dig enough, a pasture can be made here."

When a man lives by such an unrelenting philosophy he can never know defeat. Angus' words sent Cronin back to the trash barrel; he rescued his half-finished manuscript and worked harder than he had ever worked. The manuscript he had discarded was *Hatter's Castle*, a book that has been dramatized, bought by Hollywood, translated into nineteen languages, and sold well over three million copies.

There are plenty of doors open to defeat and despair. All one has to do is walk in. The way to avoid these doors is to keep working on the task which is ours to do, no matter how insignificant the task may seem. God will never let us sink as long as we find the courage to keep trying.

One of the most thrilling stories in the Old Testament is recorded in the First Book of Kings. It is an example of both victory and defeat, courage and fear. Elijah was a man of great faith: he prayed fervently and waved the flag of courage in the face of opposition. The prophets of Baal were humiliated, mocked, and defeated when the Lord answered Elijah's prayer, and the people who had worshiped pagan gods fell on their faces and said, "The Lord, he is the God; the Lord, he is the God" (1 KINGS 18:39).

Elijah never thought of defeat, for he knew God was greater than all the pagan gods. He sought to stamp out the worship of Baal by killing the pagan prophets, and they were slain by the sword. God's prophet Elijah was filled with hope. The secret of his poise and confidence is found in this little phrase, "And the hand of the Lord was on Elijah . . ." (1 KINGS 18:46).

Elijah went to the gate of Jezreel, the palace of King Ahab and his wife Jezebel, but when word reached Jezebel that her prophets had been killed by the sword, she sent a message to Elijah: "So let the gods do to me, and more also, if I make not thy life as the life of one of them by to morrow about this time" (1 KINGS 19:2). Jezebel's threat saturated Elijah's heart with fear. He forgot about God's power and the victories he had enjoyed, and ran for his life. He fled to Beersheba and left his servant and went another day's journey into the wilderness. He found a place to rest under a juniper tree and it was there that the Lord spoke to Elijah, saying, "What doest thou here, Elijah?" (1 KINGS 19:9). Elijah, in his condition of defeat and self-pity, had become a perfect example of the futility and emptiness of life in which we see only our failures and disappointments instead of our hopes and accomplishments.

I have seen a number of people do exactly as Elijah did in the face of apparent defeat: they became paralyzed with fear, and retreated into a place of inactivity. Finally, they lost their desire to live.

What happened to Elijah in the wilderness of despair? Two

things: first, God spoke to him and came to his rescue. The trouble with most people is that they do not listen to God speak when they are in trouble. Elijah was sensitive to God's voice. Second, Elijah obeyed the voice of God.

God told Elijah to "Go forth . . ." (1 KINGS 19:11). Don't just sit in your gloom—get up and do something about it! God tells us the same thing He told Elijah. If you want to win the battles of life you might as well make up your mind to get out from under the juniper tree. Then God told Elijah, ". . . stand upon the mount before the Lord" (1 KINGS 19:11). Here is the place to renew your strength. Stand before the Lord and He will sustain you. All the strength you need to break free of defeat can be yours when you stand before the Lord. A long time ago the Psalmist said, "Then they cried unto the Lord in their trouble, and he delivered them out of their distresses" (107:6). Elijah marched out of the wilderness, supported by the presence of God. This same power and presence can be ours if we make the effort to "go forth" and "stand upon the mount before the Lord."

In Australia there is a body of water called Lake Disappointment. There are times in every life when we come and stand on the shore of our own Lake Disappointment to launch our little boats. We may sail down the rivers of defeat, but with God's help we can dock our boats in the harbors of trust and faith.

I always tell people about the three roads we can take when we face defeat:

1. We can ignore defeat. Some people do this, but this is not the way to deal with defeat. If I have a tooth which is decaying, it would be foolish for me to ignore it. The sensible thing would be to go to the dentist and have the tooth treated. We can never travel the road to victory if we refuse to recognize defeat.

2. We can fill our minds with self-pity, put on garments of despair, and live by the philosophy that "there is no use to try." The people who choose to travel this road will never know the joy of looking at the sunrise after a long dark night. I know a man who has many talents. Although he has been successful in his business, he considers himself a failure. He has managed to plant, cultivate, and grow a better-than-average crop of despair and self-pity, but he needs to become sensitive to the voice of

God so he can hear Him say, "Go forth, and stand upon the mount before the Lord."

3. Finally, we can accept defeat as a challenge from God. One is never really defeated as long as he accepts the experiences of failure as opportunities to develop strong spiritual muscles. If a man sees in his disappointments a chance to weave some threads of gold into the tapestry of life, he will not be defeated for long. Jesus saw His greatest challenge in the most troubled period of His life. He turned the cruel, despairing cross into a crown of victory.

I do not see any tragedy in the fact that we do not always succeed. The tragedy is found in our failure to try again. George A. Buttrick tells an interesting story about a statue of Christ which stands in a mission at Kelham, England. The sculptor, Charles Sargeant Jagger, spent many hours trying to flash upon the screen of his mind a picture of Christ. Before he could carve a statue he had to have the idea firmly imprinted upon his mind. One day he came to the edge of despair; he was ready to admit defeat. Then, to his great surprise, the door opened and Christ stepped in and said, "Try again." That inspiration sent Jagger back to his studio where he carved a magnificent statue.

Albert J. Beveridge was unexpectedly defeated in his campaign for re-election to the senate. The disappointment did not plunge Beveridge into despair. Determined to use his talents, he began writing *John Marshall*. When that great work was completed he turned to the writing of *Abraham Lincoln*. These volumes will make a larger imprint upon the minds of men than all the contributions Beveridge may have made while serving in the senate.

Do you recall the incident in *Pilgrim's Progress* when the travelers had come to the last dark river? Hopeful was out in front, leading the way, and when he reached the midst of the river he called back these comforting words. "Be of good cheer, my brother, for I feel the bottom and it is sound." Hopeful expressed a philosophy by which we can live without fear. We may reach the bottom of life's darkest river but we do not have to give up in utter defeat. God stands near to give us the strength we need.

I remember visiting a lady who had watched her loved ones slip away one by one. A doctor, who was a friend of the family, told me, "I do not know how she has managed to stand up under such a heavy load." I knew her secret. She had touched her feet to the bottom, and she knew it was sound.

A man who came to see me told me that he was thinking of taking his life. He was worried and afraid, and his situation seemed almost hopeless. I told him frankly that I did not have the answer to his problem, but I reminded him of these words of Jesus: "The things which are impossible with men are possible with God" (LUKE 18:27). Then I asked him, "Do you really believe that God can help you find the answer to your situation?" He looked at the floor as if he were in deep thought. He began, "My mother had a strong faith. She prayed about everything. God always gave mother the answer to her problems." Suddenly he looked up and said, "Yes, I believe God can give me the answer."

"Why don't we ask Him to help you now?" I said. We prayed together, and he left with determination in his heart and a new song upon his lips. God did not solve his problems, but God opened a door that had seemed closed before we prayed.

When we come to the place in life where there are no mountains to climb, no rivers to cross, and no new roads to explore, life is empty of meaning. To accept defeat means to abandon all hope for the future on the ground that to continue would be useless, impossible, and inadvisable.

I have enjoyed the privilege of teaching at Emory at Oxford College, a division of Emory University, and I have also served as a guest professor at the Candler School of Theology. I remember a young college student who came to see me one day. He had already been notified that his work was so poor that he could not pass one of his courses and he was on the verge of being dismissed from the school. I saw that he was taking the whole situation very much to heart and was worried about what his parents would think. The one thing he absolutely had to do was to obtain a passing grade in all the other courses he was studying. The time was one week before final examinations. I told the boy, "stop brooding about the course you have failed and get busy working on the other courses. You'll never get anywhere looking back. You must press on and make the best of the situation."

I know a man who wasted the first six years of his adult life going from one job to another. He was never satisfied. He always thought he ought to have been paid more than he was getting. Finally he found it almost impossible to get a job. He became discouraged and turned to drink. That hurt his family and almost caused him to lose them. One day the man called me and asked if I would come over to see him. We talked for a long time, and among other things I told him this: "God has blessed you with a keen mind, a strong body, a pleasing personality, a wonderful family, and many opportunities. Quite frankly, you have squandered your talents, hurt those who love you, and in general made a mess of your life. You have expected too much and been willing to give too little. You have much for which to be thankful. Your parents still love you and are willing to help you; your wife and children have stuck by you. The one great thing for which you ought to be grateful is that it is not too late for you to make something out of your life. You still have time. The thing for you to do is to ask God to give you forgiveness for your failures of the past and keep your eye on the future. The future is all you have left."

A good rule to remember is that defeat need not be the final chapter in life. Human failure is often the door through which we must pass to find God's richest blessings.

Jesus appeared to the disciples early one morning as they were bringing their little boat to shore after fishing all night. They were weary and discouraged because they had failed to catch any fish. Jesus encouraged them to try again. "Cast the net on the right side of the ship, and ye shall find. They cast therefore, and now they were not able to draw it for the multitudes of fishes" (JOHN 21:6). No man is completely defeated as long as he is trying.

To allow ourselves to live in the state of defeat is to deny the power of the Christian faith. It implies that human strength and wisdom are our only sources of power; it ignores God and closes the door through which help must come. Marcus Aurelius wrote, "Man must be arched and buttressed from within, else the temple wavers to the dust." No man will be able to overcome defeat until he is able to discover a vital faith that is bigger than his sad plight.

I think of the church as God's most effective instrument in establishing His Kingdom upon the earth. No other institution is dedicated to the task of bringing humanity in line with God's divine will. The church seeks nothing for itself except to stand faithfully amid the world's hate, confusion, and evil, reminding mankind that God forgives our ugly sins, loves us unconditionally, and wishes for us spiritual peace and happiness. One thing we must never forget is that unless God is at the center of the church commanding His forces, all our efforts are of no avail.

In *Faith for Living* Lewis Mumford wrote, "And a church that taught one part of mankind to walk upright and unafraid through one Dark Age may yet summon up the power that will enable us to avert another Dark Age, or to face it, if it begins to descend upon us, with unyielding courage." Therefore, it is my unequivocal belief that the power of God is able to lead us from defeat to victory.

There are five steps we can take when the fog of defeat covers our souls, impairs our vision, and weakens our efforts:

1. We can try to regain our self-confidence. How do we go about doing this? By turning our lives over to God, by asking Him to restore our self-confidence, and by walking in faith, trusting that He will help us.

In one of my columns in the *Atlanta Constitution* I wrote a little prescription to help people forget their frets and worries and lean on the everlasting arm of God. Among other things, I said, "Say very slowly and reverently, 'God is my refuge, and underneath are His everlasting arms. I am His child and He loves me.'" I recommended that the reader say this ten times each day. It was not many days before a lady called me and said, "I have always been one to fret and worry over the least little thing. Self-confidence has been the one thing I have lacked. But your prescription works. It has helped me to face each problem with poise and confidence."

During my ministry many doors of opportunity have opened to me. I have stood at these doors and looked in with a desire to enter, yet I have felt insecure at times. I have asked myself,

"Am I prepared to do this task effectively?" One day, when I was trying to decide whether I should enter one of the open doors, I asked God to guide me. I prayed, "Am I big enough to do this job?" Before the prayer was ended God seemed to speak to me. He said, "No, you are not big enough to do it alone. But here is My hand; take it and together we will succeed." Self-confidence flows into the human soul when we take God as a partner. There are no limits to what a person can do if he marches through life with the mind of Christ and the guiding hand of God.

In the French Alps a young student was trapped for three days on the north face of perilous "Fool's Needle" in the Mont Blanc range. He was dangling from a narrow ledge when rescue workers found him. His hands were frozen and later, on a hospital bed, he told about the harrowing ordeal. "I repeated over and over to myself," he commented, "I must hold on, I must hold on at any price." He was able to keep his self-confidence by talking to himself.

I do not know of anything that will restore self-confidence more readily than reflecting upon these words of our Lord: "For God so loved the world, that he gave his only begotten Son, that whosoever believeth in him should not perish, but have everlasting life" (JOHN 3:16); and "I am come that they might have life, and that they might have it more abundantly" (JOHN 10:10). Combine these two passages in your mind. What do they mean? Sermons and books have been written on these ideas, but put in the simplest terms they mean three things: God loves me; God has provided for eternal life; God wants me to be happy and to enjoy an abundant life.

2. I would suggest that we keep our minds off ourselves. The most miserable creature I have ever known was a very wealthy man. He never married, he thought only of himself, and his life was corroded with greed and selfishness. Jesus knew that life would never blossom as long as men cultivated their selfishness; therefore He said, "For whosoever will save his life shall lose it: and whosoever will lose his life for my sake shall find it" (MATTHEW 16:25). Paul wrote, "For we know the grace of our Lord Jesus Christ, that though he was rich, yet for your sakes he became poor, that ye through his poverty might be rich" (II

CORINTHIANS 8:9). Jesus was always advising people to look beyond themselves and see the hurts of others. One day He met a selfish man and encouraged him to sell his goods and share with the poor.

George Bernard Shaw indicated that the highest joy in life is to be used for a purpose greater than self and to become a force in nature, ". . . instead of a feverish selfish little clod of ailments and grievances complaining that the world will not devote itself to making you happy."

3. We must fix our hearts on God. The Psalmist said, "O God, my heart is fixed" (108:1). It is not sufficient to forget self; we must take a positive step and find in life the purposes that take us to higher levels of living. Johnson Oatman, Jr., had this idea in mind when he wrote the last verse of that old hymn, "Higher Ground":

> I want to scale the utmost height
> And catch a gleam of glory bright;
> But still I'll pray till Heav'n I've found,
> Lord plant my feet on higher ground.

The Psalmist wrote, a long time ago, "From the end of the earth will I cry unto thee, when my heart is overwhelmed: lead me to the rock that is higher than I" (61:2). Man is never satisfied to stay on the human level. God has placed within each of us a divine spark that disturbs us until we give it attention.

When Jesus came face to face with the cross He was troubled. As soon as He was able to get His mind off Himself (and that took only a second) He prayed, ". . . not my will, but thine, be done" (LUKE 22:42). He fixed His heart on God and was content to do the work God had given Him to do. "Through God," said the Psalmist, "we shall do valiantly . . ." (108:13). Jesus said, ". . . seek ye first the kingdom of God, and his righteousness" (MATTHEW 6:33).

4. When we feel our feet touch the bottom of the dark pit of defeat, we can always look up. When a man sinks so deep in the mire of defeat that he cannot see to the sides or ahead, he can always look up.

Sir Thomas Browne talked about the fact that light makes some things difficult to see and other things completely invisible. If it were not for the darkness, the most magnificent part of God's creation would remain unseen—we cannot catch a glimpse of the stars in the heavens until night falls and darkness covers our beings.

I visited a friend in the hospital who, because of the nature of his illness, had to remain flat on his back for more than a month. It appeared to me that one would become very tired staying in one position for such a long time. I asked about this, and here is the answer my friend gave: "I have been looking around me all my life in an effort to find the material possessions that I thought would make me happy. During my illness I have discovered that a man cannot find happiness just looking around. He's got to look up." Sometimes a person finds himself on his back, looking up, before life makes any sense.

In the story of the ascension recorded in the first chapter of Acts, only those who looked up witnessed that great event. The writer of Acts tells us that they, ". . . looked stedfastly toward heaven as he went up . . ." (ACTS 1:10).

You cannot defeat a righteous man. You may make him discouraged, but his faith will cause him to look up; and when he does this, God will see that he keeps fighting, even in his despair.

5. Let us look beyond apparent defeat and see ourselves as God sees us. Then we can say, "With God's help, I can be the kind of person He wants me to be." In a rural English township the house in which a committee met and decided to send William Carey to the mission has been preserved. Outside the house some of Carey's words are inscribed on an old stone fence: "Expect great things from God; attempt great things for God." God looks beyond our faults and sees in each of us the person we could become; He saw in William Carey, a humble cobbler, a Christian giant who could lead thousands to Christ. Many of our human limitations are overcome when we give our hearts to God.

Peter was a hot-headed, impetuous, and unreliable fisherman, but Jesus did not choose him to become a disciple because of these qualities. He saw Peter's great potentialities; He saw a man who would one day stand before those who helped to crucify Jesus and preach with courage and conviction. Peter was arrested because of his preaching after the crucifixion. When questioned before the authorities Peter answered, "For we cannot but speak the things which we have seen and heard" (ACTS 4:20).

Jesus saw in Thomas a lack of faith, and skepticism, but He selected him to become a disciple because of what he could become. When the others cautioned Jesus about going near Judea, where He and His followers had met opposition, it was Thomas who said, "Let us also go, that we may die with him" (JOHN 11:16).

God is counting upon us to do our best. An unknown author wrote:

> No matter what others are doing, my friend,
>   Or what they are leaving undone,
> We are counting on you to keep on with the job
>   Till the very last battle is won.
>
> We are counting on you to be faithful,
>   We are counting on you to be true.
> Yes, others may work, or others may shirk,
>   But, remember—we are counting on you.

Charles Wellborn described an experience he had while he served as a soldier in Italy during World War II. While driving through a town that had been devastated, he and his comrades noticed a little boy crying bitterly as he sat near a house that was almost destroyed. Investigation showed that the little fellow's family had been killed and, though little Tony was only nine years old, the soldiers decided to take the lad with them. They made him the company mascot and a uniform was cut down to fit him. Tony felt that he was a part of the company. He loved the soldiers and they loved him.

One day the order was given that all refugees had to be turned over to a central authority. This meant that little Tony had to go. When Charles Wellborn explained to Tony that he would have to leave, he reminded the lad that he had been a good soldier and good soldiers had to obey orders. That night, when the company stood retreat, Tony stood by the captain, receiving his parting salutes from his buddies. As the notes of the bugle died away and the rays of the sun sank behind the mountains, Tony turned toward a waiting jeep. Before he reached the jeep, however, Tony the soldier again became Tony the little boy. He ran back with tears streaming down his face and grabbed Charles Wellborn around the waist, sobbing, "Don't you see, I can't go! I can't go! I belong to you!"

When we see ourselves as God sees us, we belong to Him. Many of us need to come back and sit at the foot of the cross and look into the face of our Saviour and say, "I want to be the kind of person You see in me. I am leaving the old life of futility and defeat. I belong to You. I belong to You!"

11

When You Think You Are Down

THE ANSWERS TO the perplexing problems that plague humanity are in the hands of God. I deal with problems of defeat, gloom, disappointment and sorrow in the lives of people almost daily. The one conviction which grows stronger each day in my life is the fact that God is never defeated. Often I am at a loss to give people an easy answer to their problems, but if there is no answer within my reach I always say without hesitation that "God will see you through." I am fully convinced that God never isolates us from divine help. The church always has a word of courage and hope to offer.

As a freshman in college I had an old car, and in spite of its age it was very dependable. One day I saw an automobile with a "For Sale" sign on it. It looked much better than the car I was driving, and the owner offered to trade even with me. Since I liked the looks of the car, I traded with him. I barely got home in the car that day, and, next to algebra, it gave me more trouble than any other thing during my entire freshman year. I took it to a dependable mechanic and he advised me, as discreetly and as gently as he knew how. "Young man," he said, "if I were in your place, I'd take that thing to the nearest junk yard, and if they would give me anything for it I'd take it. If they were not interested in buying it, I'd just park it somewhere in the yard and slip off and leave it."

Discreet words of wisdom and advice to one who has fallen heir to his own folly are often needed in this world. But not all problems are as trivial as an undependable automobile. Everyone faces trouble and despair at one time or another.

I have stood in hospital corridors and heard competent physicians say to anxious loved ones, "I'm sorry, there just isn't anything else we can do." I have seen gloom and hopelessness settle upon the hearts of those who knew the end was near. There comes a time when a physician must admit that he is defeated. Yet in the midst of the dark night the church offers a word of hope and courage.

The storms of life are often turbulent, but through the mist and fog we can see the warm lights of the harbor. We can never drift beyond His love and care. We may not be able to sail around many of the storms of life, but with God's help we can sail triumphantly through them.

Our world is infested with evil. War, oppression, crime, and a good deal of the suffering we see remind us that all is not well between man and God. A casual glance at any daily newspaper reflects the awful state of confusion and disorder in which we find ourselves. Our juvenile courts are busy, our prisons are overcrowded, our hospitals are filled, and our divorce courts have waiting lists. In spite of so much ovewhelming evidence of the grip that evil has on humanity, I am filled with optimism. The world is not a mechanical monster that is rampant and out of control; God still has His hand on the throttle and His foot on the brake. He is still the supreme Ruler of the universe.

Do you remember when the disciples were low in spirit because they could not understand why Jesus had to leave them? The future looked pretty hopeless. Jesus said unto them, "In the world ye shall have tribulation; but be of good cheer; I have overcome the world" (JOHN 16:33). He was facing the realities of life, but at the same time He assured the disciples that they could be victorious.

Helen Keller wrote, "Keep your face to the sunshine and you cannot see the shadows." This is a beautiful philosophy, but it is not because my face is constantly toward the sunshine that I am an optimist. I see the shadows. I know something about the heartaches that people endure. I hear almost daily the sordid tales of the so-called other side of life. My optimism is not found in the ugly and evil marks that humanity leaves on the canvas of time, but in the inexhaustible love and measureless mercy of God. I must confess that I am appalled at man's ability to blot and stain his soul, but my optimism is rooted in God's ability to redeem us from the sins of the past.

Someone has written that ". . . optimism is the consciousness of hidden reserves." The consciousness of hidden spiritual resources has inspired many stumbling followers of Christ to get up and walk again.

Paul had every right to be discouraged. He kept going, not because of the progress he was able to make—because at times progress seemed nil—but because of the hidden reserves he felt within his soul. Jesus moved optimistically and steadily toward the cross, not because it looked like victory, but because He was fortified with the consciousness of hidden reserves.

A woman called and asked me to pray for her. She has brought up her family and now lives alone. "I am not able to work," she said, "and all I do is sit in my room, day after day. I am often lonely and depressed but when I remind myself that I am not really alone, God makes me happy." I advise a lot of people to take courage because God's grace is deeper than the stains of sin, His strength is stronger than our burdens, and His love is wider than our sorrows. My faith in God gives me an inner compulsion to defy the evil that is so evident and proclaim the optimism that I feel within. With God, you and I can overcome the world.

The arm of the Christian church is almost two thousand years long. There are some voices that tell us the church has exhausted its usefulness, that it speaks to generations that have marched across the stage of life and are now in the halls of eternity. Is the church shouting empty phrases? Are our creeds and doctrines little more than sounding brass or tinkling cymbals? Are we uttering bits of charming philosophy and fascinating psychology with little or no eternal significance? Are we preaching an euphemistical gospel? Do we soothe the sins of society and pat the sinner on the back, assuring him in his sins by saying, "That's nothing to worry about—everybody else is doing it," or "Forget it, God will understand"? Do we speak for God or for man? That is the crucial question.

Has the church lost its usefulness? If we proclaim the view of men—men gripped with prejudice, haunted with fear, and stifled with selfishness—then the church has betrayed God and our proclamations serve only to soothe the sins of man and cover up the ugly stains of the soul. The church must speak for God; it must proclaim God's message to our generation. Such a message is a timeless and an inexhaustible source of power. It may come to us in the form of a stinging revelation as we stand before God with the secret sins of the soul exposed. When the truth of God grips a man's life it is as refreshing to his soul as a bubbling spring of fresh water is to the parched lips of a thirsty man in the midst of a hot desert.

History serves as a reminder that the rumbling feet of armies that once caused fear to throb in human hearts are now silent—yet Christ continues to live. Empires that sought to snuff out the Christian church have crumbled, civilizations have come and gone, world power has shifted from one nation to another —but Christ remains, and He is our only hope. God stalks through history, leaving for every generation a path to follow out of the darkness of confusion.

What is the business of the Christian church? We are to proclaim the truths of God. What are the great truths of God? (1) God revealed Himself to man through Jesus Christ. It is an amazing truth to discover that God wanted you and me to know what He is really like. (2) Jesus Christ died for you and me. Why? I cannot say; I only know that He died for our sins. (3) Our sins can be forgiven. We can be redeemed persons. We are not sentenced to carry through life the heavy load of guilt which is the fruit of our sins. (4) Life is eternal. Life is not the beginning of the end; it is an endless journey.

Our job must never be less than proclaiming to a weary and broken humanity that life can be a thrilling adventure. God loves us with an unceasing love. If we speak for God, ours must be a redemptive gospel.

There is a story about a Christian missionary who served God in the Orient. He understood the people, knew their language, held their respect, and taught them the love of God. A large Western industry offered the missionary a salary of ten thousand dollars a year to serve as their representative, and he refused the offer. The company then made a new proposition: "We will pay you fifteen thousand dollars to represent us." He declined this offer. "What about twenty-five thousand?" Again, he turned it down. The company suggested, "Our last offer is fifty thousand dollars a year!" The missionary replied, "I am sorry, I cannot do it." "Tell us why!" the company begged. "Is the salary not satisfactory?"

"Oh, yes," the missionary responded. "Your first offer is much more than I am being paid now—but your job is too small."

The task of the church is the biggest job in the world. Sometimes we forget this or get sidetracked. We often become involved in petty interests. We dabble in politics; we present logical lectures on current events; we promote little ethical systems. We want to run the church our way. We are disturbed if the parking lot is not convenient, yet our souls are numb when we hear of the uncounted millions who never have enough to eat. We want someone to do all of the work at the church and keep things in readiness for us, but when someone calls for a pledge we are perfectly willing for someone else to do the giving. We want the air conditioning just right in church—if it is too warm or too cold we are likely to become indignant—yet we remain apathetic toward our neighbors who show little or no interest in God's Kingdom.

Ours is a big job. We must tell the human race that there is a way out of prejudice and sin. Outside and inside the church there is a weary multitude searching for life's true purpose. We dare not do less than tell a broken humanity about the love of God and His willingness to forgive their sins.

I have a friend who normally greets me by asking, "What do you know?" I generally respond by saying, "I don't know much." Actually I know some things that ought to be shouted from the housetops around the globe. I know God loves us, forgives us, and cares for us.

On the night Jesus was born, shepherds were keeping watch over their flocks. When the angel of the Lord appeared and the glory of the Lord shone round about them, they were filled with fear. To soothe the fears of the shepherds the angel said, "Fear not: for, behold, I bring you good tidings of great joy, which shall be to all people" (LUKE 2:10). Indeed, the birth of Christ was good news! The news of the church is the best news because it rings with a victorious truth that can be heard through all eternity.

Alfred Tennyson, upon arriving at a friend's home, asked, "What is the news?" The hostess replied, "There is only one piece of news I know: Christ died for all men." "Well," said Tennyson, "that is old news, and good news, and new news." There is no greater news than to discover this truth for one's self.

Jesus was born in an obscure village. Little is known of His early life, but suddenly He broke the silence and moved quickly to perform God's work. He gathered a small band of disciples around Him and set out to proclaim God's truth. One of His disciples denied Him, one betrayed Him, and all disappointed Him at one time or another.

When the shadow of the cross became evident to our Lord, it looked like defeat for Him and His disciples and triumph for wrong. Yet Jesus possessed a spirit of undaunted hope, and after the resurrection the disciples caught that same spirit. The church was small in number, but as Bishop Arthur J. Moore says, "It was blessed with a magnificent courage and confidence. It saw the worst and believed in the best."

Paul dreamed of going to Rome to win that mighty empire for Christ. What a fantastic hope! Rome was the heart of a magnificent empire ruled with an iron hand. The marching legions of Rome would, by any earthly standard, cause one to classify Paul's hope as sheer foolishness. How could one little Jew, with his frail body, armed with no credentials, and having no organization, expect to shake the mightiest empire on the face of the earth? He was coming to Rome armed only with "the gospel of Christ" (ROMANS 15:29). But the gospel of Christ was everything to Paul. He wrote to the Philippians, "For to me to live is Christ . . ." (PHILIPPIANS 1:21).

When Christ grips a man's life and when he lives under His persuasion the mountains that were once too high can be scaled and the valleys that were once too deep can be descended.

Rome may have been a challenge for Paul, but it was no challenge for God, and Paul moved not in his own strength but armed with "the gospel of Christ." Again Paul wrote to the Philippians, "I can do all things through Christ which strengtheneth me" (PHILIPPIANS 4:13). Through Christ he could even shake the very foundations of the Roman Empire.

Is there anything in your life which ought to be mastered, and which you are unable to conquer alone? Are there sins that need to be forgiven? God will forgive them. Are there evil habits that need to be broken? With God's help you can triumph over them. Do you need help in loving your enemies, in praying for those who despitefully use you, and in forgiving those who have wronged you? Relationships can be restored, and you can be free from sin's grip. That is the best news I know.

You may wade through some murky waters of adversity, you may climb some rugged mountains of sorrow, you may sail some turbulent seas of disappointment, you may walk through some dark valleys of loneliness, you may stumble down a rocky path—but victory can be yours! Everywhere Jesus assures us. He tells us not to be afraid and He bids us face each new day with perfect trust in His wisdom, power, and goodness.